Art Quilt Collage

*a creative journey in
fabric, paint & stitch*

Deborah Boschert

C&T PUBLISHING

Text and photography copyright © 2016 by Deborah Boschert

Photography and artwork copyright © 2016 by C&T Publishing, Inc.

Publisher: Amy Marson

Creative Director: Gailen Runge

Editor: Lynn Koolish

Technical Editor: Del Walker

Cover Designer: April Mostek

Book Designer: Christina Jarumay Fox

Production Coordinator: Zinnia Heinzmann

Production Editors: Jessica Brotman and Jennifer Warren

Illustrator: Freesia Pearson Blizard

Photo Assistant: Carly Jean Marin

Instructional photography by Diane Pedersen, unless otherwise noted

Published by C&T Publishing, Inc., P.O. Box 1456, Lafayette, CA 94549

Library of Congress Cataloging-in-Publication Data

Names: Boschert, Deborah, author.

Title: Art quilt collage : a creative journey in fabric, paint & stitch / Deborah Boschert.

Description: Lafayette, CA : C&T Publishing, Inc., [2016]

Identifiers: LCCN 2016003476 | ISBN 9781617452840 (soft cover)

Subjects: LCSH: Quilting. | Collage. | Art quilts.

Classification: LCC TT835 .B6297 2011 | DDC 746.46--dc23

LC record available at https://lccn.loc.gov/2016003476

Printed in China

10 9 8 7 6 5 4 3

41 50 61 74

contents

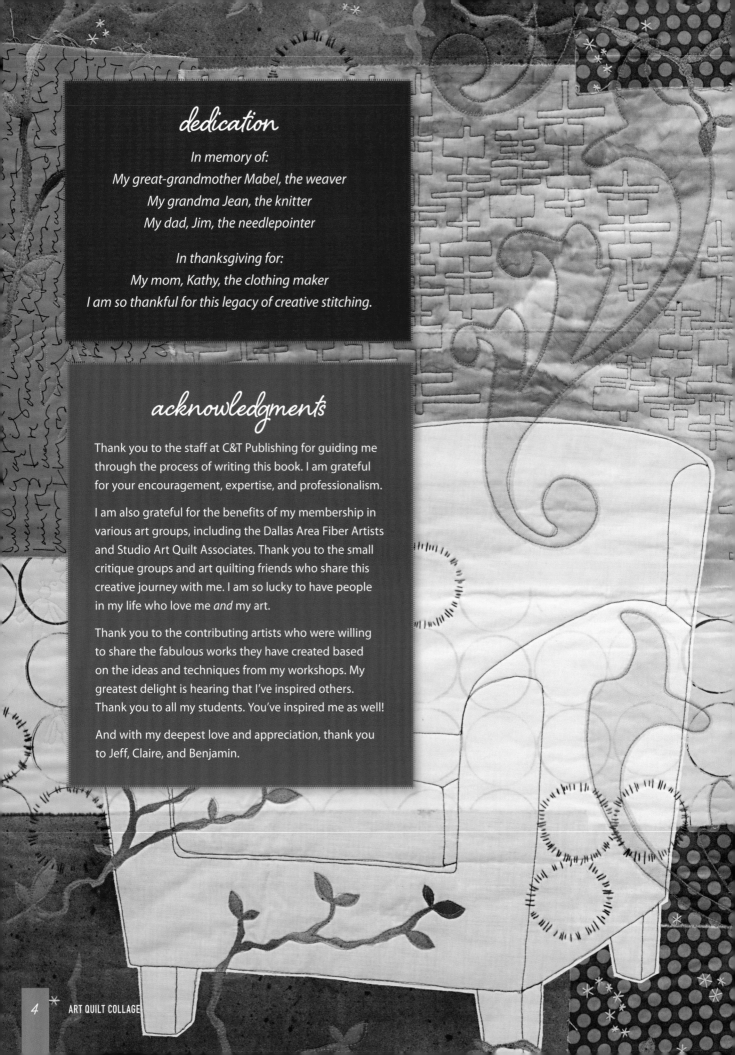

dedication

In memory of:
My great-grandmother Mabel, the weaver
My grandma Jean, the knitter
My dad, Jim, the needlepointer

In thanksgiving for:
My mom, Kathy, the clothing maker
I am so thankful for this legacy of creative stitching.

acknowledgments

Thank you to the staff at C&T Publishing for guiding me through the process of writing this book. I am grateful for your encouragement, expertise, and professionalism.

I am also grateful for the benefits of my membership in various art groups, including the Dallas Area Fiber Artists and Studio Art Quilt Associates. Thank you to the small critique groups and art quilting friends who share this creative journey with me. I am so lucky to have people in my life who love me *and* my art.

Thank you to the contributing artists who were willing to share the fabulous works they have created based on the ideas and techniques from my workshops. My greatest delight is hearing that I've inspired others. Thank you to all my students. You've inspired me as well!

And with my deepest love and appreciation, thank you to Jeff, Claire, and Benjamin.

introduction

Just recently I spent over an hour searching my studio for one specific piece of fabric. It was a short length of printed burlap from a beautiful Asian import store in Wiscasset, Maine; I remember splurging on it while visiting friends. Nine years later I hadn't used the fabric, but I knew it was tucked away in one of my drawers. I was forced to clean the floor of my studio closet in order to find the proper drawer, but when I found the burlap it was exactly as I remembered it. I was designing a new art quilt and the burlap was the perfect addition. The quilt is on my design wall, and I am loving what's happening with the combination of fabrics, shapes, and stitching so far. Plus I am loving remembering that trip to Maine: coffee with my friends, the collection of treasures on the porch outside the shop, and the beautiful drive along the coast. (I am also loving the bonus of the newly cleaned studio closet!)

When you create artwork, you bring your whole self to the process. All your favorite colors and textures, your memories, and your experiences. The skills you've mastered and the skills you're still working on. The materials you purchased just yesterday or years before.

After years of creating art quilts, I've settled into a process of building layers of design with fabric, paint, and stitching. It allows room for all those experiences and memories, plus favorite techniques and materials. I am delighted to share this process with you. It's a formula for creating a captivating composition and then adding details with layers of paint and stitching. Along the way, you'll make small and large changes. You'll consider options for adding your own personal symbols and unique details. The formula is completely flexible and encourages you to find a way to create original work that you love.

SEE WHAT HAPPENS

Some of the chapters include short exercises called "See What Happens." This is the mantra I always bring into the studio with me. It suggests that every part of the creative process has potential for discovery.

Whether you are cutting, sketching, stitching, layering, stamping, painting, writing, or just exploring, the outcome of every creative effort is full of possibility. The end result may not become a great piece of art, but it may lead to a new idea that leads to the best work you've ever created!

After each of the See What Happens exercises, there are several questions to consider. The questions may point toward fresh possibilities. They can help identify what's exciting and what's drudgery—which is different for everyone. Your answers can point toward new ideas and take you to the next step in the creative process.

HOW TO USE THIS BOOK

We all approach reading a new book differently. Some sit down and read from cover to cover. Some flip through and look at the pictures for inspiration. Others jump around, picking and choosing what they want to do. What you do depends on your personality, and some of it depends on where you are on your art quilting journey.

Take a look at the list that follows and see how you might want to use this book.

- Read through the chapters to get a sense of the process of building a quilt with layers of fabric, paint, and stitching.

- Do the See What Happens exercises to … well, see what happens.

- Review the supplies and materials needed for creating a layered art quilt. Maybe you need to visit a quilt shop or art supply store (not that you *need* an excuse to go shopping). Maybe you'll just need to gather the supplies from your drawers and cabinets.

- Discover new ways to look for inspiration and learn how to apply it directly to your creative process.

- Study individual sections for the techniques that are most interesting to you, such as printing with found objects, new embroidery stitches, ideas for chopping up fabric, or creating texture with machine stitching.

- Put a sticky note on The Eight Design Guides (page 22) and the Design Checklist (page 30) so you can easily refer to them.

- Maybe even make a copy of the design checklist and put it up on your wall to refer to during your current creative endeavor.

- Check out Personal Symbols (page 41) to explore the very personal possibility of including symbols in your artwork.

- Gather lots of tips for working with fusible web, including cleaning it off your iron. (Don't tell me you've never gotten fusible on your iron; we all have.)

- Learn techniques for finishing the edges of an art quilt.

- Check out innovative suggestions for titling your art quilts.

- Read through the five parts of the Practice Exercise to get a sense of the process of creating a layered art quilt.

- Create your own art quilt by working through the five-part Practice Exercise.

- Take bits and pieces and make them your own. The ideas and techniques in this book translate easily to mixed media and other types of fiber art.

- Keep it on the bookshelf to refer to later. I hope you'll find new inspiration each time you open it.

- Share it with your friends.

Hibiscus, 12″ × 12″ This quilt includes commercial prints and fabrics, plus painting with stamps and stencils. It is stitched with both thread and embroidery floss using free-motion quilting and hand embroidery. A well-supplied studio ensures endless possibilities.

in this chapter

✳ Learn about supplies for art quilts, including typical items such as fabric and thread, plus unexpected supplies such as sponges and spray bottles.

✳ Begin to envision how layers of fabric, paint, and stitching come together to create an art quilt.

✳ Consider when to use what you have and when to upgrade your supplies.

✳ Remember that the most important tools are your imagination and the world around you.

After years of creating art quilts and developing my own personal style, I've found my favorite materials, tools, and techniques. They help me work efficiently and make the process enjoyable. (Enjoyable is important!) There are many ways to create art quilts, but the following are the supplies I use regularly.

When choosing and gathering supplies, don't get overwhelmed. There are so many fabrics—with variations in color, pattern, quality, fiber content, price, and availability. It's the same for paint, thread, embroidery floss, and every possible notion in the sewing aisle at the fabric store, not to mention all the options online. Don't worry about it. Just go with what you have, or make the best, easiest choice, and then spend the rest of the time creating.

FABRIC AND BATTING

Quilting cottons are great for art quilts. In addition to cotton, any fabric is fine as long as it's interesting and fits the concept of the art quilt you're creating. Sheer fabrics, upcycled clothing, vintage linens, lace, and home decorator fabrics are all possibilities.

For small art quilts, felt works great as batting. It's stiff, firm, flat, and easy to stitch through. Wool-blend felt is lovely, but polyester felt is fine. For larger quilts, an 80/20-blend batting is a good choice. Hobbs makes my favorite battings.

DON'T MELT YOUR FELT!

If you are using unusual materials such as organza, tulle, polyester felt, or other delicate fabrics, be sure to test how they react to your iron. Some fibers melt or burn. Adjust your iron temperature accordingly and/or use a protective cloth over those fabrics when pressing.

developing your fabric stash

Art quilters have access to an enormous variety of fabric. A painter buys a tube of red paint and it's just red; if a quilter needs red, she can choose from stripes, solids, large-scale florals, or tiny geometric prints. There are fabrics printed with tomatoes or poppies or even fire trucks. Don't forget a shiny red satin or a nubby red burlap. It can be tempting to stock up on all these options and build a big stash of possibilities.

Be careful—too many choices can be overwhelming. When a particular color or type of fabric is running low in your stash, consider buying a few half-yard cuts to expand your stash just a little. If I'm working on a project and I can't find just the right fabric, sometimes I force myself to work with what I have. This can lead to exciting and unexpected solutions. Sometimes it's best to shop specifically for a project rather than collect fabrics without a plan.

FUSIBLE WEB

Art quilts are easily constructed using heat-activated fusible web that secures one fabric to another. There are several brands available, and all include simple instructions with their packaging. Lightweight fusibles work best for fabric collage. Misty Fuse is my favorite.

It's handy to have a nonstick surface to use when applying fusible web to fabric. Parchment paper or Silicone Release Paper (C&T Publishing) works well and can be disposed of after several uses. Teflon-coated fiberglass sheets are long lasting and can be cleaned and reused.

BASIC SEWING SUPPLIES

Of course you need an iron and a sewing machine. It's nice to have an iron with a Teflon soleplate. If you end up with fusible web on your iron—and you will—a Teflon soleplate makes it easier to clean. Use a spray bottle to create steam while pressing fabrics rather than filling the iron with water. (Just spray water directly on the fabric and then press with a hot iron.)

Any sewing machine with a simple straight stitch and the ability to drop the feed dogs for free-motion quilting is fine. You also need pins, a tape measure, and a seam ripper.

CUTTING TOOLS

Three sizes of scissors will cover most tasks: large for cutting big chunks of fabric, small for cutting detailed fabric shapes, and tiny for hand embroidery. Use a craft knife for cutting foam for stamps and freezer paper for stencils. The Fiskars Fingertip Detail Knife is super convenient because you hold it like a pencil and it swivels while cutting. A rotary cutter, ruler, and cutting mat are useful when measuring fabric or cutting straight lines. A rotary cutter can also be used to slice long, graceful curves. It's nice to have decorative rotary blades to create interesting edges.

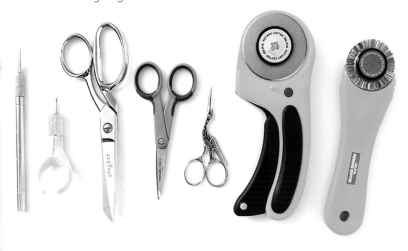

NEEDLES AND THREAD

All kinds of thread work fine for art quilting—inexpensive or high-quality cotton, poly, blend, and so on. It's nice to experiment with a variety of weights, colors, and fibers.

Hand-Embroidery Thread, Needles, and Thimbles

There are many options for hand embroidery. DMC brand embroidery floss is most readily available, comes in lots of colors, and is consistent in quality. Try stitching with just three strands of embroidery floss or use all six.

Perle cotton comes in various sizes or thicknesses and wonderful colors. The higher the number, the finer the thread. DMC also makes a variety of perle cottons. Beautiful hand-dyed variegated perle cotton is available from independent artists.

The Jeana Kimball Size 8 Embroidery/Redwork needle is perfect for hand embroidery. It's long and sharp and has a large eye. It easily accommodates three strands of embroidery floss but also works with all six strands. Larger gold-tipped needles work well for thicker fibers such as perle cotton.

Thimbles are quite personal. If you plan to do a lot of stitching, it's definitely worth finding one that you like. A leather coin thimble is pliable and almost molds to the shape of your finger.

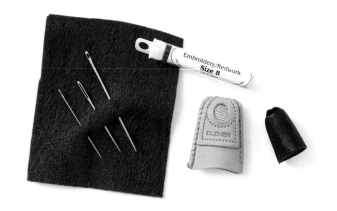

PAINT, PENS, AND MARKING TOOLS

Paint

Surface design (page 50) can be added to fabric using acrylic paint. Look for an inexpensive paint that comes in a lot of colors and has a consistency that isn't too thick or too thin. Use whatever paints you have and feel free to test other options. Spray dye is a fun option for surface design too. Textile paints are available as transparent, opaque, or metallic. (Textile paints are simply acrylic paint with a special textile extender mixed in.) Recycled Styrofoam meat trays make excellent paint palettes.

Pens for Surface Design

When adding marks such as handwriting or sketched outlines to fabric with pen, use Pigma Micron pens. The widest width is numbered 08 and measures .5 mm. The brush-tip Pigma Micron pen also makes a lovely mark.

NOTHING LASTS FOREVER

When your fabric pens no longer make a nice dark line, throw them away! (Or repurpose them for writing on paper.) When paint dries up, throw it away. If you forget to clean a sponge or brush and it's caked with paint, throw it away. It's a hassle to try to work with tools that are old and disagreeable. You deserve better.

Marking Pens

When you need to mark a line for stitching, there are several options. The best bet is a blue disappearing-ink pen with marks that dissolve easily with water. There are others that slowly disappear when exposed to air. If the disappearing-ink pens don't show up on dark fabric, try a chalk pencil. Chalk pencils come in a variety of colors. Some quilters even use a sliver of soap to mark lines. Be sure to test your selected marker on similar fabric to make sure the line really disappears.

Sponges, Brushes, and Brayers

A foam stencil brush is an awesome tool for paint application. It's great for applying paint to stamps and for filling in stencils. Foam stencil brushes come in several sizes. When a more typical brush is needed, just use whatever is on hand. Nothing special. When you're printing on fabric, a brayer is great for applying paint to a surface such as a large foam stamp or a piece of bubble wrap. If you're working with an item that is too big to apply paint to using a foam stencil brush, a brayer is a good option.

DESIGN WALL

It's important to take a good look at your work throughout the design process, so a design wall is an essential tool. Viewing your work on a vertical space is different from viewing it on a table in front of you. In addition, a design wall gives you the opportunity to step back and assess how the art quilt looks from a bit farther away. Colors, details, and patterns may stand out or get lost, and you can edit as needed.

The most basic design wall may simply be a piece of batting pinned or taped to the wall. In-progress works can be pinned to it. A more useful and permanent solution is a sheet of insulation from the hardware store. The sheets are usually 4′ × 8′ but can be cut down as needed. Cover the insulation with batting or felt and attach it to the wall. The biggest advantage of insulation sheets is that you can easily pin into them. This is great for hanging in-progress works. My design wall is often covered with scraps of fabric, shopping lists, cool postcards, or other items that need attention.

UNEXPECTED TOOL

A lint roller is an excellent tool to keep in the studio. It's perfect for picking up stray hairs, threads, and fibers from finished art quilts.

FIND TOOLS THAT WORK

As you create and develop your own personal style, you'll develop preferences for supplies and tools. There are pros and cons to all materials and supplies. The most expensive is not always the best. What works for one person may not work for another. I recommend starting with what you have and trying other options as you explore new techniques.

As you try various techniques, you'll find situations that require different or better tools. If it's a technique you want to explore further, consider upgrading your tools. Always try working with what you have at first.

DON'T FORGET

The best creative resource is the most readily available—it's just the world around you. Grab your camera and snap pictures of anything inspiring or even just odd and interesting. Read about events, people, and ideas. Keep a notebook where you can sketch and make lists. Seek entertainment that is funny, witty, provocative, educational, or deeply emotional. Build relationships with people who want to know about you and your artwork. All of this informs your personal style and influences your artwork.

Memories of sidewalk cafés in Belgium

Amazing stone pattern at Fort Niagara

Three chairs in different shapes and colors; a tiny peek of a leafy branch

Such unexpected shapes in this pink flower seen on a walk at Mom's house

Because I'm from the Sunflower State—Kansas!

Someone thoughtfully arranged the chairs at this pizza joint in Austin.

Dr. Seuss-like plants at Diamond Head National Park

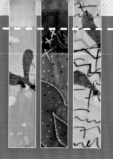

inspiration
and fabric selection

Blue Chair Mantra, 60″ × 24″

The inspiration for this quilt came from the idea of rituals. After moving many times in my life, I try to make a ritual of clear thinking and calm breathing even when the situation is stressful. Sometimes that means I need to just sit quietly and be aware of everything around me. The inspiration for this quilt may not seem obvious. That's the amazing thing about creating art; you can take anything at all, interpret it creatively, and express your ideas in unique ways.

in this chapter

✳ Consider resources for inspiration.

✳ Think about creating a series of art quilts inspired by similar colors, fabrics, symbols, or themes.

✳ Explore the possibilities of the fabric layer of your art quilt by selecting a fabric palette.

✳ Review how many and what fabrics to choose for your art quilt.

✳ Discover inspiring colors, patterns, and compositions in a favorite photo in the See What Happens exercise.

very art quilt begins with a nugget of inspiration and some fabric. It's easy to say that inspiration can come from anywhere. But how do you translate it into art? It's easy to fall in love with fabrics, colors, and patterns. But how do you narrow down the choices and set yourself up for success?

EMBRACING INSPIRATION

Inspiration is that moment when you notice your pulse racing just a bit. Or you gasp with unexpected delight. Or an idea keeps swirling around in your brain. These are signs of inspiration. They can help direct the design of an art quilt in many ways. The following can be sources of inspiration:

Being inspired by these ideas does not mean you want to create an art quilt that is a direct representation of the ideas or imagery. It means taking bits and pieces—the colors, shapes, imagery, and mood—and using them to guide the creative process.

- A line from a song or poem, especially if it evokes imagery or emotions

- A favorite piece of clothing, maybe the ripped knee on a pair of jeans

- Vacation memories: the sights, people, food, or experiences

- The curvy tail of a house cat or the expressive eyebrows of a pet dog

- The colors in your garden, even after the growing season is past and everything is dry

- Big emotions—the good ones and the not-so-good ones

- An interesting piece of fabric, product packaging, or a movie poster

- The sights and sounds you encounter during a walk through your neighborhood

Sources of Inspiration

The following are some concrete examples of ways to identify inspiration and translate it into an art quilt.

FOCUS FABRIC

Choosing a focus fabric—by looking for a piece of fabric that makes you gasp or that you can't stop studying—is a great source of inspiration. It's possible to build an entire art quilt around a piece fabric. Focus fabrics work best if they include a variety of colors—that will help you choose coordinating fabrics, paints, and thread colors. If the fabric is a large-scale print, you may use only a tiny bit because busy prints can distract from the overall design. Or you might use big, bold chunks. Focus fabrics guide and inspire the rest of the art quilt through their color palette, pattern, and mood.

Savory Scatterings, 12″ × 12″

The batik fabric with the green fern and earth-tone background was the focus fabric for this quilt. All the other fabrics were chosen to coordinate and complement the color story from that fabric.

PHOTOS

Taking inspiration from a photo is entirely different than recreating the photo as an art quilt. When a photo catches your eye, look at the colors in the photo and think about what fabrics would make interesting representations of those colors. By examining the shapes and the composition of the photograph, you can make design choices inspired by those elements. Look for lines and patterns that would make interesting motifs for stitching. Even the mood of the photo might offer potential for creative expression.

PRETTY PICTURES

Magazines are often full of beautiful images. Flip through magazines looking for colors, shapes, settings, or compositions that are inspiring. Remember, you're not looking for images to recreate—you're just looking for inspiration.

Red Yucca, 10½″ × 9″

This archway marks the entrance to a walking trail in our neighborhood. I snapped this picture because the red yucca was blooming like crazy. It's one of my favorite Texas plants. It was fun to create this small quilt inspired by the photo. The color palette references the blue sky, the red of the yucca, the dark green trees, and a combination of the white stones and the tan pathway. I abstracted and simplified the photo in many ways, picking and choosing interesting shapes and patterns.

THEME

It's a fun challenge to create an art quilt based on a specific theme. Theme can be an inspiration. You may want to create a quilt with an artichoke, a sunflower, or a sand castle as a theme. A special event or gift-giving opportunity makes a good theme. Themes can be broad or narrow. Don't feel too constrained by a theme; just use it as the very first spark of inspiration. Build fabrics, colors, shapes, and stitching motifs around any of these ideas.

OBVIOUSLY!?

Actually, the theme or inspiration of your art quilt does not have to be obvious to the viewer. The theme may become obscured or altered as you create. A nugget of inspiration may get you started, but you may find yourself on a different path as you progress. That's totally fine.

WORKING IN A SERIES

Sometimes after completing an art quilt inspired by a particular color palette, photo, or theme, you may find yourself eager to continue exploring the same images, patterns, and ideas. This is a great opportunity to create a series.

Working in a series lets you really dig into the potential of a particular technique, composition, theme, image, or any other element in your work. It also allows you to develop a cohesive group of quilts while developing your own personal style as you find ways to use the same sources of inspiration in different ways.

Artists sometimes wonder when an idea has exhausted itself. If you still find a particular nugget of inspiration interesting and you are eager to find new ways to create with the same idea, you should! Some artists build their entire career around a familiar element. At other times, a series may include only a few pieces.

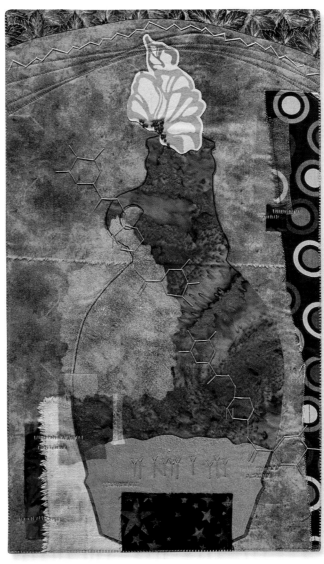

Sugar Maple, 20˝ × 12˝

For a group challenge, I needed to create a quilt exploring the theme "sweet." It took me a long time to settle on the sugar maple tree and a maple syrup bottle as interesting imagery that fit the theme. After I settled on the idea, the quilt was a delight to design and stitch. I even included the chemical structure of sugar.

GATHERING A FABRIC PALETTE

Begin each project by gathering a fabric palette. Your inspiration may be a fabric, photo, theme, or something entirely different. With that in mind, begin pulling fabrics from your stash. Stack and sort fabrics until you have a pleasing collection that includes a variety of colors, patterns, and textures. It's a good idea to include some solid fabrics that can be enhanced with surface design (page 50). When considering prints, look for variety, but everything should work together. You can even include some unexpected fabrics such as decorator fabrics, upcycled clothing, or a bit of felt or velvet.

The purple batik with green accents in the center acts as a focus fabric for this palette.

How Much Fabric?

When creating a small art quilt (no more than 20˝ on any side), it's great to work with two or three fat quarter–sized pieces of fabric, plus several scraps (3˝–12˝). Working with a fabric palette that includes 12 to 18 different pieces of fabric creates lots of options. You may not use all of them, but you'll have an inspiring palette to work with.

DON'T GET DISTRACTED

As I design an art quilt, I draw only from the fabric palette I've gathered. I've already made design decisions about the fabrics, and I'm not going to be distracted by anything that might be in my stash usually. This helps keep the creative process moving forward and relieves the agony of deciding between too many options.

IDEAS ABOUT COLOR

I'm not a fan of complex color theory. It seems overly specific, academic, regulated, and calculated to me. While some artists use a color wheel to inform design decisions, here are some alternate ideas to consider when making choices regarding color.

Interesting top half of the picture filled with bright green leaf shapes

Don't be afraid of lots of color.

Pop of green

What Do You Like?

Pay attention to color combinations that catch your eye. Notice paint schemes on the houses in your neighborhood, interesting clothing, billboards, flowers, and product packaging. Inspiration is everywhere. Take photos and make note of color palettes you like, and consider exploring them in fabric. Simply choosing colors because you like them is perfectly fine. Explore whatever combinations of colors give you a jolt of excitement and make you want work with them.

Refer to Your Inspiration

Working with a focus fabric, photo, or theme will help guide your fabric color choices. If the focus fabric is full of cool tones of blues and greens, stick with that range as you choose other fabrics for the art quilt. If your inspiration photo is a beach scene with one tiny red umbrella, you have a great opportunity to use a red pop of color.

Think about Contrast

When gathering a fabric palette and thinking about color, make sure there are enough options to create contrast. Without enough contrast, everything can look muddy when viewed from a few steps away. Gather some dark, dark fabrics and some light, light fabrics. Consider deep, dark navy blue and pale, light lavender. (Unless you want to create a subtle, mostly-one-color art quilt that might suggest quiet simplicity—in that case, you don't want too much contrast.)

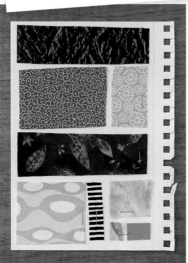

The photo is from a hike in Hawaii. I love the graffiti on the sign and the lush greenery. It's a great photo to use as color inspiration. I chose several fabrics while studying the palette of the photo. I clipped swatches to visualize how they would work together, thinking about the proportions of color in the photo. It's mostly green, so I cut large chunks of dark, medium, and light greens. The brown from the sign is translated into a leafy brown print as a nod to the scene. A groovy yellow print fits the words on the sign. There is a small black-and-white sticker on the sign, so a sliver of black-and-white striped fabric adds a pop of contrast. Two small blue squares reference the hues in the graffiti. The tiny lavender flower peeking out from the green leaves gets the smallest square of fabric.

Unusual composition with feet and legs. Where were we going?

Photos are great resources for building a design for an art quilt. This exercise will help you break down a photo into its individual inspiring elements. If you wish, you can take those elements and use them as inspiration for an art quilt. But this exercise can also stand on its own as a way to explore thinking about design in new ways.

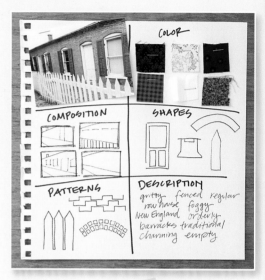

1. Choose a photo you love. It could be from a magazine or from your personal collection. Pick a photo that is interesting because of the color, composition, or details. Focus on the elements of the photo rather than the content of the photo. A super-cute picture of your beloved pet is great to put on the refrigerator, but it's not suited to this challenge. A better choice would be a picture of an interesting building or landscape from a recent adventure.

2. Divide a page in your sketchbook (or a plain piece of paper) into 6 sections.

3. Cut out or print out the photo and tape it into one of the sections.

4. Label the remaining sections "Color," "Composition," "Shapes," "Patterns," and "Description."

5. Go through your fabric stash to find samples that match the colors in the photo. Look for a variety of solids, patterns, and hues. Cut tiny swatches of each fabric. Tape, staple, or glue them in the section marked "Color."

6. In the "Composition" section, make a very simple thumbnail sketch of the basic composition of the photo. Eliminate all the details and focus on the basic shapes and how they are organized within the frame. Make more than one sketch if you want to.

7. Look for isolated shapes in the photo. Draw several of those shapes in the "Shapes" section.

8. Notice the patterns in the photo. These may be textures or backgrounds. The patterns may seem unimportant, but they can still be sources of inspiration. Simplify what you see into a set of repeated lines and draw them in the "Patterns" section.

9. In the "Description" section, write a few adjectives to describe what you see in the photo. Consider words that might have both positive and negative connotations.

I chose a photo of a brick barrack behind a white picket fence. It's a pretty simple photo, but I found several interesting details.

ASK YOURSELF

- Which section was the easiest to fill in?
- Which section was the most difficult?
- Are you eager to make an art quilt using this photo as inspiration?

- Can you imagine reproducing your sketched patterns using machine or hand stitching?
- What did you notice in the photo that was unexpected?
- Did the photo help you choose one fabric over another?

- There are no right or wrong answers—the answers will give you clues about your approach to designing art quilts.

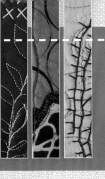

design *and* composition

Haze and Hope, 39″ × 37″ This quilt languished on my design wall for months. The design didn't come together easily. I had pieces and parts, but they didn't work together. Two things helped me move forward. First, a thoughtful friend visited my studio and we considered several options. Second, I sliced several inches off the bottom of the quilt. Creating this quilt reminded me to be patient, ask for help, and edit.

in this chapter

✳ Discover the potential of composing using the Eight Design Guides as templates.

✳ Consider composition tricks and tips such as rotating, combining, and editing.

✳ Strengthen your composition skills with the Design Checklist.

✳ Begin the Practice Exercise by gathering a fabric palette, choosing a Design Guide, and exploring possible compositions.

✳ Create eight quick fabric sketches in the See What Happens exercise.

The design and composition part of creating an art quilt is the most demanding … and the most rewarding! It is full of tweaking, testing, auditioning, agonizing, experimenting, exploring, searching, and scrutinizing. But it's also full of potential, excitement, positive energy, and surprises. Sometimes this process happens over just a couple of hours. Sometimes it takes days. (Or even years.)

Try many options and make small decisions along the way, until you've created a composition you love. You may take some wrong turns before you settle on a successful composition, but that's part of the process. In fact, figuring out what doesn't work is as important as figuring out what does work. Then the challenge is to avoid repeating the wrong turns and remember to incorporate the successes in the future.

THE DESIGN PROCESS

Before you dive into the creative process, consider some ideas about design and composition.

You may have heard of the Elements and Principles of Design. They are academic ideas for creating good visual art. I refer to them occasionally, but sometimes they just create confusion. Rather than focusing too much on academic standards of "good design," you can ask yourself lots of little questions throughout the creative process. Let's set aside the traditional elements and principles and explore my Eight Design Guides.

The Eight Design Guides

You know that feeling of staring at a blank page and not knowing how to begin? The Eight Design Guides will get you over that hurdle. Think of them as templates, blueprints, or diagrams of possibilities.

The sketches allow you to envision many possible colors, fabrics, lines, and shapes within the composition. That's why they are simple line drawings, with no color or detail to distract you from your own ideas. Each Design Guide can work on its own as a beautiful, spare, simple composition, or it can act as a foundation on which to build additional details.

LANDSCAPE

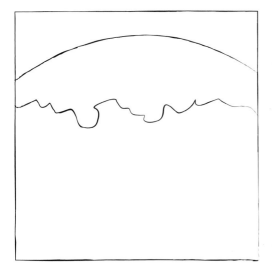

This composition is simply horizontal strips. Each strip is a different width, and the edge of each strip suggests some kind of landform: a hillside, a grassy field, or a forest in the distance. Does it have to be a true landscape? No. It's just a composition guide for cutting and arranging fabric.

Promising, 8″ × 8″

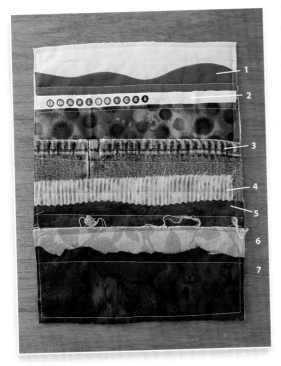

using edges

Each strip in a landscape composition can have a different edge treatment. So many potential design opportunities! Here are some examples to try. (Of course, you could use these interesting edge treatments with any art quilt, not just a landscape composition.)

1. Use a rotary cutter to cut a graceful curve suggesting rolling hills.

2. Use the selvage. It's fun to highlight the colorful dots occasionally combined with text.

3. Use the hem of a recycled garment, like the worn edge of a pair of jeans.

4. Rip the fabric along the grain.

5. Cut with a decorative rotary blade; this blue fabric was cut with a zigzag blade.

6. Embrace fraying edges—fabric that has been tossed around in your stash or that just came out of the wash may have interesting textures.

7. Cut a sloppy, jagged edge.

GRID

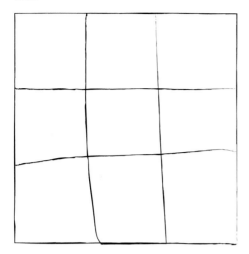

This composition is a throwback to traditional quilting and the Four-Patch block. Place fabrics in a grid format, or place shapes in a regular grid-like pattern. The grid concept can work at any size from a simple 4 × 4 grid to a much larger checkerboard-style wall quilt.

Bountiful, 8˝ × 8˝

THIRD PLUS

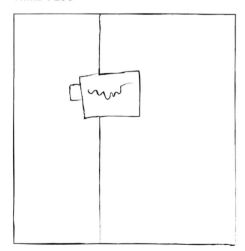

Fill one-third of the space with one fabric and the remaining two-thirds with another fabric, and then place an interesting detail on the line between the two fabrics. (Or slightly above or below the line. Or slightly to the left or right of the line.) This composition works horizontally or vertically. The detail (the "plus") can be expanded in many ways. It could be a shape or symbol. It could be an additional line that crosses over the composition. It could be a small arrangement of fabrics with lots of texture and color.

Seedlings and Stones, 8˝ × 8˝

SYMMETRICAL

This arrangement of shapes is the same on the left and the right. The shapes in this thumbnail are just suggestions. The leaf shape could be a tree or a bird or a rectangle or any other focal element.

Spirited Soaring, 8″ × 8″

seeing symmetry

Would you believe this is the patio of an ice cream shop in Minnesota? The beautiful symmetry of the building is inspiring. The string of lights hanging from the trees throws off the symmetry just a tiny bit and adds whimsy and ambiance. The color palette, composition, and variety of shapes in this photo could be the inspiration for an art quilt.

BREAK IT UP

As you add details to a symmetrical composition, throw off the symmetry just a bit so the design doesn't become too predictable.

MAGIC THREE

River Gathering, 8″ × 8″

Groups of three are pleasing to the eye. Abstract or realistic shapes work well in this simple format. Cut a shape in slightly different sizes and arrange the shapes at different levels within the design space. They could be flowers, teacups, stars, or simple squares cut from a fabulous fabric.

ONE AMAZING LINE

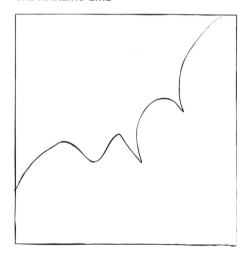

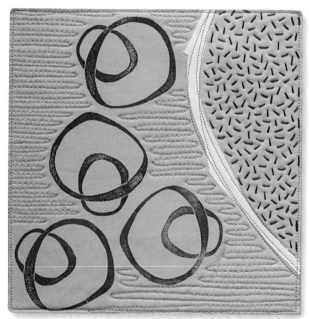

Drift and Detour, 8″ × 8″

Yes, you could make an entire art quilt by focusing on just one line that is interesting to you. It could be curvy or jagged. It might bisect your composition in the middle or sweep across the top. The line could even be a specific representation of something: a word, a profile, a skyline.

DANCING GRID

Take all the organized shapes from the simple grid design, add some different sizes and colors, and then rearrange them in a thoughtful way. It's not chaotic. There is rhythm, pattern, and organization to it, like a dance.

Tide Pool Guide Tool, 8″ × 8″

transforming designs

What if you finish an art quilt and it doesn't look like the original Design Guide you started with? Who cares! The purpose of the Design Guides is simply to provide a starting point in the creative process. After you begin cutting fabric and creating interesting compositions, feel free to make big or small changes that lead you in interesting directions.

MODULAR

A thoughtful stack of shapes can create a fantastic composition. Many traditional still-life paintings are modular designs. The elements in the design connect to each other both physically and visually with common colors and shapes.

Rising Reverie, 8″ × 8″

Design Guide Variations

The Eight Design Guides offer many possibilities. Pick and choose and mix and match as you like.

HORIZONTAL OR VERTICAL FORMAT

The Eight Design Guide sketches are square, but they can easily translate to horizontal or vertical formats. A vertical landscape (page 23) in an extreme proportion could be very dramatic. Imagine a tall, skinny beach scene with a dramatic sunset where the sky stretches up above the water in beautiful colors. The Grid (page 24) could be stretched out into a wide, interesting configuration of shapes. One Amazing Line (page 26) might be a single dynamic line from bottom to top, or it could be a long horizontal horizon.

SIZE

The Design Guides also work in any size. Create tiny 3″ × 3″ collages with small pieces of beautiful fabrics. Large art quilts with a variety of fabrics, surface design (page 50), and large and small stitched motifs might also be inspired by the Design Guides.

ROTATING THE DESIGN GUIDES

Many of the Design Guides can be rotated. Third Plus (page 24) works fine horizontally or vertically. One Amazing Line (page 26) has potential for variation by rotating the line across different sections of the design area. An abstract composition using the Modular or Dancing Grid Design Guide (page 27) could work in any configuration. As you're designing, rotate your composition to see if different elements stand out in different ways.

COMBINING THE DESIGN GUIDES

Several of the Design Guides work well together. The Landscape Design Guide (page 23) makes a wonderful background for Magic Three (page 26), especially if the three elements are trees or flowers or houses. One Amazing Line (page 26) can be complemented by a smaller modular (page 27) section. The small detail in the Third Plus Design Guide (page 24) can be a mini grid.

Spring Suggestion, 12″ × 12″

The background for this quilt is inspired by the Landscape Design Guide (page 23). It's simply three horizontal strips: the navy with the green bars, the blue middle sky, and the dotted upper sky. The three bare tree trunks are an example of the Magic Three Design Guide (page 26).

turn it around

I have a friend who creates beautiful abstract art quilts incorporating large fields of mostly solid colors. One day our small critique group looked at one of her in-progress pieces that wasn't working. We discussed possibilities, including slicing it up and reconfiguring the elements. Someone suggested rotating it 90°. She repinned it to the design wall and we were stunned by how different it looked. Suddenly the unresolved shapes that appeared to be floating in the original configuration seemed grounded and powerful. Especially with abstract work, it's fun to rotate the design and "see what happens." Even with realistic art, there are sometimes elements within the design that could be rotated to improve the design.

DESIGNING IN STAGES

As you're composing, you may leave an area unfinished, planning to fill it out with another layer of design later in the process. For instance, if you are using the Grid Design Guide (page 24), you can leave some sections of the grid empty and plan to add paint or stitching rather than fabric. The Symmetrical Design Guide (page 25) is perfect for continuing the design with stitching that complements the fabric elements. During the composition process, it's completely okay—in fact, sometimes it's essential—to leave some areas unresolved. The fabric is only the first layer of an art quilt.

THE ONGOING DESIGN PROCESS

It's time to just dive in! Pull together an inspiring palette of fabric. Choose one of the Design Guides and begin auditioning, arranging, testing, exploring, and designing with chunks of fabric. The Practice Exercise (page 33) is a more structured exploration, but if you want to get started with your own ideas, use the following key steps.

Key Steps for Creating a Layered Art Quilt

1. Gather inspiration and fabric.

2. Design, edit, compose. Repeat as needed.

3. Fuse the fabric layer.

4. Consider adding personal symbols (page 41).

5. Consider adding surface design (page 50).

6. Plan and add stitching by hand and by machine.

7. Finish.

MAKE A NOTE

Mark this chapter with a sticky note! The Eight Design Guides and the Design Checklist are resources you'll be referring to throughout the design process.

WHAT IS THE DESIGN CHECKLIST?

As you compose, you should always be editing and auditioning possibilities—it's part of the process. After creating many art quilts and developing my own personal style, I find that some of this comes naturally, but an organized format helps me decide if everything is working.

HOW TO USE THE DESIGN CHECKLIST

The Design Checklist is divided into five sections:

- BALANCE
- HARMONY
- REPETITION
- EDGES
- FINE-TUNING

Each section includes questions to ask about your design. The questions prompt you to examine all the details in your composition. As you answer the questions, you may find areas that could be changed, improved, edited, or polished. After each question are some suggestions to consider.

There are no right or wrong answers. Some questions will not apply to what you are working on. Some of the suggestions may not make sense at all. That's fine! The Design Checklist gets you thinking and analyzing. Some of the suggestions may contradict each other, but they are designed to give you lots of options and possibilities. You will find the Design Checklist useful at many stages in the design process. You may also focus on different questions and options from the Design Checklist as you work on different projects.

Asking and answering the questions on the Design Checklist can guide you to creating something you really love!

design checklist

BALANCE: Elements Are Distributed in a Pleasing Way

Is the visual weight balanced—either symmetrically or asymmetrically?

Yes. Shapes, colors, and details are distributed throughout the design.

No. But the dominant area is dynamic and interesting and I like it.

If you are not happy with the visual balance, consider the following options:

- [ ] Adding or removing details
- [ ] Exploring horizontal, vertical, or radial symmetry and adding small details to break the symmetry
- [ ] Creating a focal point, or moving or removing a focal point

Are there areas that feel empty?

Yes. They create resting spots for the eye.

Yes. I'm planning to fill them with other techniques in the next design stage.

No. The empty areas are an important part of the design.

If you don't like the emptiness, consider the following options:

- [ ] Making some shapes larger to fill the space
- [ ] Adding a painted pattern or stitching
- [ ] Enhancing the background so the area doesn't feel empty

HARMONY: All Elements Work Together

Are any shapes or colors standing out?

Yes. I want them to be the center of attention.

No. Everything works together.

If you don't like the way the shapes or colors are standing out, consider the following options:

- [ ] Choosing colors from the same family to create a visual connection, such as blues, greens, and purples, or reds, oranges, and yellows
- [ ] Changing the color, size, or placement of an element to create more or less emphasis
- [ ] Giving the focal point more importance by creating an outline or frame around it, or reducing the focus on an element by covering it slightly with another element

Is there a focal element?

Yes. It's arranged effectively.

No. The design works without a focal element.

If you want to add a focal point, consider the following options:

- [ ] Picking something unexpected as a focal point
- [ ] Complementing a focal point with interesting details
- [ ] Simplifying the design

Are the design elements overlapping?

Yes. They blend together thoughtfully.

No. Each item fills its own space.

If you don't like the placement of the design elements, consider the following options:

- [ ] Overlapping elements even more to create a connection, or separating them for greater distinction
- [ ] Creating depth with some pieces in front of others—try variations.
- [ ] Adding stitching or paint that will connect elements to the rest of the design

Is there enough contrast between all the elements?

Yes. Each element stands on its own.

No. But everything blends beautifully.

If there isn't enough contrast, consider the following options:

- [ ] Adding a line of paint or stitching to emphasize an area
- [ ] Changing the background color to enhance contrast or to minimize contrast
- [ ] Adding a small pop of color

REPETITION: Elements Appear More than Once

Are elements visually connected by shape or color?

Yes. They help draw the eye around the design.

No. Individual elements get attention because they are unique.

If you don't have the visual connection that you want, consider the following options:

- ☐ Using the same fabric in two or three different areas of the design
- ☐ Choosing paint, fabric, and embroidery floss in the same color
- ☐ Continuing or repeating a line or shape from one area of the design to another

Are elements repeated throughout the design?

Yes. They create pattern and rhythm.

No. Each element is unique.

If you don't have pattern or rhythm, consider the following options:

- ☐ Using odd numbers of shapes
- ☐ Creating a visual triangle by repeating three elements in different areas of the design
- ☐ Arranging elements in a regular order to create a sense of affinity or calm compatibility

EDGES: The Outside Edge Works

Do any lines draw the eye off the edge of the design?

Yes. But other lines bring the eye back into the frame.

No. Everything visually keeps the eye within the frame.

If the eye is being drawn out of the design, consider the following options:

- ☐ Placing elements to draw interest into the design, not off the edges
- ☐ Creating shapes that point to areas of interest
- ☐ Adding a border that would visually frame the design

Could the composition be improved by cropping?

Yes. I could slice off a section to make the design better.

No. The size and design are working.

If you don't like the composition, consider the following options:

- ☐ Taking a picture and testing cropping possibilities on your phone or computer
- ☐ Making two L-shaped pieces of paper or cardboard to try out various crops by holding them up to the piece
- ☐ Finishing at an unusual size or with irregular edges

Note: If you choose to crop, make sure nothing important will get cut off when you finish the edges.

FINE-TUNING: All the Details Work Together

Is the design visually chopped in half?
Are individual elements chopped in half or visually divided in half?

Yes. It complements the design.

No. There is variety that creates energy.

If you don't like the composition, consider the following options:

☐ Moving elements around to add interest

☐ Examining where lines and shapes intersect and adjusting as needed

☐ Reviewing possibilities for symmetry or asymmetry

Could the design be improved if it were rotated?

Yes! Wow!

No. It definitely works best in the original orientation.

If you aren't happy with the orientation, consider the following options:

☐ Rotating the entire piece

☐ Rotating elements within the design

☐ Flipping elements from one side to another

☐ Grounding elements at the bottom of a design or letting them float

Are there any issues that need attention?

Yes. I have plans to address them as I go.

No. Nothing detracts from the visual impact of the work.

If there are issues, consider the following options:

☐ Examining frayed edges, jagged lines, and smooth curves and making sure everything works

☐ Deciding how you will address thread tails, knots, varying stitches, and other related details

☐ Examining the work from close up and from far away, to see what might be changed

Do you love it?

Yes. I'm excited to move on to the next design stage.

No. I'm still working on the details.

If you don't love it, consider the following options:

☐ Taking a break and coming back with fresh eyes later

☐ Asking your friends for thoughts and suggestions

☐ Moving ahead and planning your next piece of art

Inspiration, Fabric, and Beginning Design

Throughout the book, the Practice Exercise will lead you through the process of creating an art quilt. Each chapter will introduce new materials and techniques as you build up layers of design.

This is not a pattern! It's a guide and a set of examples. In each part, there is room for you to make your own individual design decisions. You can recreate a quilt from the examples, you can tweak and adjust some small parts, or you can set off on your own entirely!

MATERIALS

✳ **Fabrics:** see Step 2.

✳ **Felt:** approximately 14″ × 18″

✳ **Fusible web:** approximately 2 yards

✳ **Poster board or large sheet of paper:** approximately 14″ × 18″

---

1. Choose an inspiration for your art quilt (see Embracing Inspiration, page 15). This may be a focus fabric, a photograph, a theme, or some other nugget around which to build your art quilt. A focus fabric is used for this project.

Focus fabric with several shades of blue

2. Gather options for your fabric palette (see Gathering a Fabric Palette, page 18). Try to gather 12 to 18 fabrics in a variety of colors, including solids and prints.

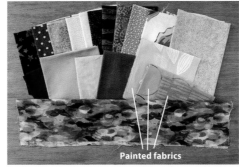

Painted fabrics

This fabric palette includes a range of prints, solids, and some fabrics that have already been painted.

3. It's helpful to have a design window that will help you visualize the finished size of the quilt. From the poster board, cut a window measuring 12″ × 16″.

4. Prepare your workspace with your fabric palette, sketchbook, felt batting, cutting area and tools, design window, and fusible web.

5. Choose one of the Eight Design Guides (page 22) and make a few quick thumbnail sketches of possible compositions. The Symmetrical Design Guide is used for the Practice Exercise.

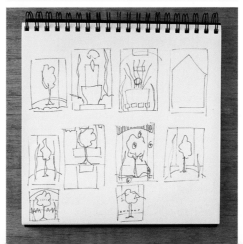

6. Begin arranging fabrics on the felt. Fold and scrunch the pieces to envision different designs. If the fabric is too large, cut chunks to audition and arrange with other chunks.

Focus fabric may be too hidden? Feels very vertical; could be broken up a bit with more horizontal details. Nice mix of prints.

This "horizon" line would be more interesting as a gentle curving line. Background fabric too plain? Too many dotted fabrics; need variety.

Background fabric too busy? The two side rectangles seem to be floating. Top half feels light in value; bottom half feels dark.

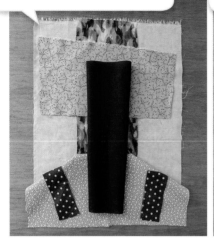

Three design ideas

7. Settle on a composition and the fabrics to be included. Remember that more details can be added later. This is simply the first layer of design.

8. Cut the chosen fabric into chunks the approximate size required for the design.

9. Prepare the fabric by ironing fusible web to the back of each fabric piece (see Construction, page 36).

10. Cut the final shapes that will make up the art quilt.

11. Put the shapes up on the design wall (page 12) to evaluate. Pin the fabric pieces in place if necessary. Refer to the Design Checklist (page 30) as needed.

12. When you are happy with the arrangement, take the pieces to the ironing board. Smooth the fabric flat on top of the felt, making sure each piece is exactly where it belongs. Fuse the pieces in place.

That's it for now. The Practice Exercise continues in Part 2 (page 47).

Here's a quick exercise to familiarize yourself with the Eight Design Guides (page 22). You will make what are almost like sketches, but with fabric. There is no substitute for just grabbing the tools at hand to "see what happens." The idea is not to create finished small art quilts; it's just to get a feel for cutting, composing, and following the format of the Design Guides. (You may wish to add details and stitching, which is great!)

Can you identify each of the Eight Design Guides?

1. Cut 8 pieces of felt, each about 4½″ × 4½″.

2. Cut a 4″ × 4″ window from a piece of card stock to use as a visual size guide.

3. Arrange all 8 pieces of felt in your design area.

4. Gather prefused fabrics that work together; scraps about 10″ × 10″ work well. Small prints or solids work best, as each composition is so small.

5. Grab a pair of scissors and begin slicing and chopping, working quickly to create a simple rendition of each of the Eight Design Guides.

6. Either work on one at a time and then move on to the next, or bounce back and forth between compositions. Don't worry about precise shapes or edges. Embrace spontaneity.

7. As you're composing, use the 4″ × 4″ window to check that each design works within the frame.

8. As you work through the designs, occasionally step back and see if anything jumps out. Does something look odd? Does something look awesome?

9. Make small improvements as you go, but this activity should be done fairly quickly and spontaneously.

10. Fuse the final designs to the felt bases.

11. Trim each block to 4″ × 4″.

12. Keep the collection as your own Design Guide reference.

ASK YOURSELF

■ Which composition came together most easily?

■ Do any of the compositions still feel unresolved?

■ Did you wish you had more fabrics or colors to work with? Or did you use even fewer than planned?

■ Did you find yourself working slowly and deliberately? Or quickly and spontaneously? Do you like to create abstract designs? Or do you incorporate realistic shapes and images?

■ Again, there are no right or wrong answers—just think about your preferences as you continue through the book.

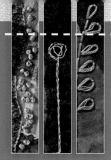

construction

Driving, 20″ × 12″

When I was in high school I worked in a clothing store at the local mall. I had a Ford Maverick and often drove home after dark. I remember driving past cornfields and over long passes of highway. Driving gave me a feeling of independence.

in this chapter

✳ Discover the amazing versatility of fused appliqué.

✳ Learn tips and tricks for working with fusible web (even how to clean it off your iron).

✳ Think about how to build and manage a fused fabric stash.

In August 2004, when I lived in Maine, my mom came to visit and we drove to New Hampshire to participate in a workshop with art quilter Melody Johnson. It was a great adventure to share with my mom, and it started me on the path to developing my own personal style as an art quilter. Melody taught me how and why to create art quilts using raw-edge fused appliqué.

I expanded my fusing vocabulary, methods, and materials beyond Melody's techniques over the next several years. We are longtime email friends, and she has watched me develop, knowing that I built my artistic voice on techniques learned at that original workshop. That's why artists teach: to give their students the skills, experience, and inspiration to create their own work. My hope is that this book will provide you, the student, with techniques to develop your own artistic voice.

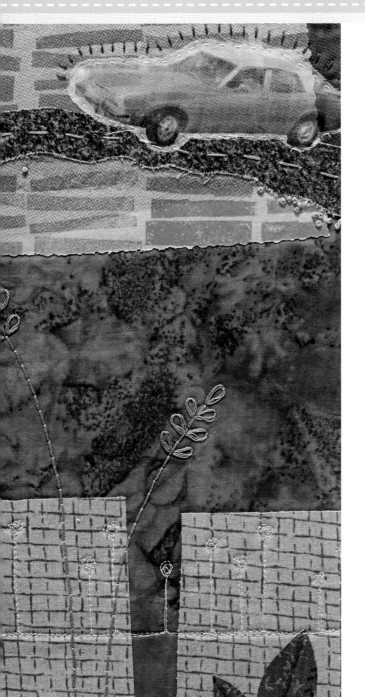

RAW-EDGE FUSED APPLIQUÉ

The process of creating an art quilt using the raw-edge fused appliqué technique is very straightforward. Where a painter dips her brush into paint and creates a shape on a canvas, an art quilter cuts a shape from fabric and fuses it down. Ready for another color and another shape? Simply cut it out from a different piece of fabric and fuse. No measuring. No sewing. No seam allowances.

A variety of shapes cut from pre-fused fabric.

Working with Fusible Web

Rule #1 for working with fusibles is to follow the manufacturer's instructions. Different brands and types of fusible web require different iron temperatures and timing. Generally, the iron should be dry—no steam.

USING FUSIBLE WEB

1. Apply the fusible to the back of your fabrics, following the manufacturer's instructions.

2. Peel off the backing if there is one.

3. As you're building a quilt, tack and fuse the fabrics lightly at first. Do this with a lower heat setting and just a quick swipe with the iron. This will allow the pieces of fabric to be gently peeled up if you change your mind.

4. When the design is completely finalized, fuse everything as indicated in the manufacturer's instructions.

NONSTICK SURFACES

It's important to have a flexible, portable nonstick surface for preparing fabric with fusible web and when composing a fused design. Parchment paper from the grocery store is one option. You can also purchase Silicone Release Paper (C&T Publishing) in handy 8½˝ × 11˝ or 17˝ × 22˝ sheets. Parchment paper and Silicone Release Paper can be reused a few times before they lose a bit of their nonstick quality. There are also large, slick Teflon-coated flexible sheets of fiberglass, known as appliqué pressing sheets, that can be used many, many times.

Any of these options will protect your ironing surface. A great feature of these sheets is that you can construct small fused fabric compositions on the nonstick surface and then peel them off and add them to a larger art quilt.

MORE THINGS TO KNOW ABOUT USING FUSIBLES

- Make sure the fabric is cool and dry before applying fusible.

- Use a nonstick surface both under the fabric and on top of the fusible web to avoid getting sticky fusible on the ironing board and the iron.

- Wait until the fabric and fusible are completely cool to peel off the release paper or Teflon sheet. Seriously, wait. It makes a huge difference.

- First peel up a corner to make sure the fusible has fully attached to the fabric.

- If you're using a fusible with a paper backing, always remove all the backing paper. There's no need to keep it on for stability or storage, but you can reuse the release paper.

- Cut the fusible just a tiny bit smaller than the piece of fabric you are preparing. This avoids sticky bits of fusible hanging off the edges. Trim off any unfused edges or other areas. This will help you avoid inadvertently cutting into an unfused area and leaving a section of the fused shape unattached.

- BUT … if you have an unfused edge that is interesting, use it as a design element. Just be aware that the unfused portion won't fuse to the background, but it can easily be stitched down.

- Don't be stingy. Fuse more fabric than you think you'll need. The scraps can be used in fabulous future projects.

- Clean Teflon sheets with a vegetable brush or bathroom scrubby.

- With light-colored fabrics, sometimes it's difficult to tell which side has the fusible web. It will feel smoother and look shiny in the light, but if you still can't tell, place the fabric between two sheets of Silicone Release Paper and press. The side that sticks to the release paper has the fusible.

- Test a small piece of prefused fabric with the felt or batting you plan to use for your art quilt. Make sure the iron temperature is set so the fusible fuses but the poly felt doesn't melt. Sometimes when you are fusing to batting with scrim, the layers seize up a bit. Try adjusting the heat level or use a different batting.

Fused Fabric Stash

A stash of prefused fabric is like a shelf full of paint or a box of crayons. After fabric is prepared with fusible, it can be cut into any shape or size and fused to another piece of fabric to create an art quilt.

Sometimes I use prefused fabric and sometimes I prepare fabric with fusible web as I go, or I combine the two. As you create art quilts with fused fabrics, your stash of fused leftovers will grow. Sometimes you'll need a particular fabric that hasn't been fused, so you'll prepare it, use it, and add the scraps to your stash.

WHAT IS TOO SMALL TO SAVE?

I save almost every small scrap of prefused fabric. Even tiny bits or long narrow strips can be incorporated into art quilts in interesting ways. All my scraps are simply tossed in a big plastic bin. It's not very organized, and I have to dig through it to find what I need, but it works for me.

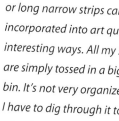

what about the raw edges?

Fabric is woven and has texture. Raw-edge appliqué is just that, raw-edge. Sometimes it frays. Don't worry. Showing and highlighting those features is part of the beauty of creating with fabric. There is no need to turn edges under or cover them with stitching—although you can if you like. It's your art.

Layers of Fused Fabrics

With fused appliqué, the fusible web is ironed to the wrong side of the fabrics you've chosen as your fabric palette (page 18). The prefused fabric is cut and incorporated into the design of the quilt. Sometimes a quilt will include several layers of fused fabrics. A bird may be fused to a tree that is fused to the background fabric. That's three layers. Realistically, you will find it difficult to stitch through more than five or six layers of fabric, and the quilt will be stiff and bulky in the areas with more layers. If you find you do want to include more layers or you want less bulk, cut away the insides of the shapes that are under the uppermost fused shapes, leaving about ½˝ of fusible around the perimeter of the shapes.

Prefused fabric pieces can be rearranged, and you can add and subtract shapes throughout the design process. When the design is finalized, fuse everything directly to the felt or batting. After that, it's difficult to unfuse or peel off fabric shapes.

ALONG THE WAY

Remember to refer back to the Design Checklist (page 30) as you're composing with your prefused fabric shapes. The questions in the Balance, Harmony, and Repetition sections will provide guidance as you compose your quilt.

FUSED BACKINGS

After completing the design with fabric and adding layers of paint and stitching, you will fuse an additional piece of fabric to the back of the art quilt. Because the quilt top and the backing are fused to the batting, stitching isn't really necessary to hold the layers together. But stitching can add another layer of design, texture, and dimension (see Stitching, page 61).

CLEANING SMALL ART QUILTS

Small art quilts created with the materials and techniques recommended in this book should not be washed in a washing machine. If an art quilt is dusty, it can be gently cleaned with a dry cloth or lint roller. Small marks or stains can be addressed with a damp cloth and a tiny bit of gentle laundry soap.

REMOVING FUSIBLE WEB

Stray Fusible on Fabric

Inevitably, some fusible web will end up where it doesn't belong. It might be the ironing board cover, a piece of fabric, or the surface of your art quilt. You may be able to scrape it off with your fingernail or an old credit card. If that doesn't work, place a piece of tinfoil over the unwanted fusible and press with a hot iron. The fusible should remelt and grab onto the foil. Let it cool and then carefully peel up the foil, lifting the fusible with it. Repeat as needed with clean pieces of foil.

Stray Fusible on Your Iron

If you end up with fusible web on the soleplate of your iron, there are a few tricks for getting it cleaned up. Keep an old dish towel hanging over the end of your ironing board. When the soleplate gets sticky, firmly drag the iron over the dish towel several times. The nubby texture of the towel may help remove some of the sticky mess. You can also try firmly dragging a hot iron over a used dryer sheet. Iron cleaning pastes are also available.

BONUS SMALL ART QUILTS

At the end of a project, I often have prefused bits of fabric in a pile on my studio table. Before I clean up and redistribute everything back where it belongs, I might create a couple of small art quilts using the scraps from the previous project. A big part of the design process is finding colors and fabrics that work together, so that's already been done. Sometimes I use a composition similar to the original piece, or I'll refer to the Eight Design Guides for a fresh idea. This feels like a quick, fun no-brainer exercise, but sometimes it turns into a fully realized piece that I'm thrilled to add to my body of work. It's also a sneaky way to create a small series of related artworks.

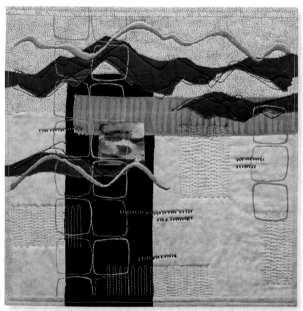

Catching Reflections in the River, 12″ × 12″

After preparing the Practice Exercise for this book, my studio table was strewn with scraps. I created this quilt with the same fabrics, using an entirely different style. I took inspiration from the Third Plus Design Guide (page 24) and the One Amazing Line Design Guide (page 26). I used only a tiny bit of the focus fabric, but it still sets the mood for the piece. I loved adding the stamped squares as surface design. They were created with an empty toilet paper tube. (See Surface Design Techniques, page 57.)

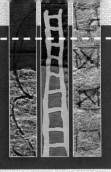

personal symbols

Yellow Ladder, 12″ × 12″

When I created this quilt, I thought the ladder was simply an interesting shape. Throughout the process of stitching the quilt, I thought more about what a ladder might symbolize: challenge, adventure, ascent, and growth.

in this chapter

✳ Think about how personal symbols can be included in your artwork.

✳ Explore possible sources for developing and defining your own personal symbols.

✳ Learn how to add symbols to your art quilt.

✳ Consider adding a personal symbol to your Practice Exercise.

✳ Contemplate the shape, stories, and significance of a possible symbol in the See What Happens exercise.

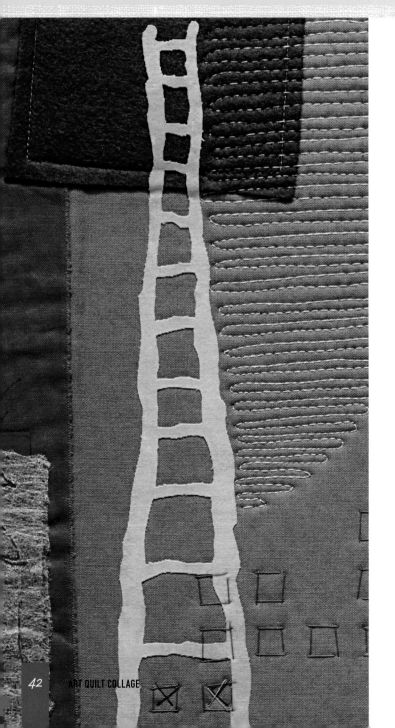

A few years ago, I was on a tight deadline to create an art quilt using green, blue, red, and yellow. The color palette was not enough to inspire me. I needed something else to explore: a theme, an image, a story. I remembered an impressive sculpture I'd seen at the Modern Art Museum in Fort Worth, Texas. It's a ladder installed in a dramatic alcove. The ladder is nearly three stories tall. It's delicate, crooked, and expressive. Aha! I had an image as inspiration to combine with the color palette.

Since then, I've incorporated ladders into art quilts in various ways. The ladder means different things to me at different times. I assume it means different things to different viewers. It's become part of my personal collection of symbols.

FINDING AND DEVELOPING PERSONAL SYMBOLS

Notice Everything Around You

Anything can be a personal symbol. The meaning doesn't have to be obvious. It only matters that it means something to you. As you're going through your day, make a mental note of things that jump out at you. Consider what they could symbolize. Maybe you get caught at a railroad crossing on your morning commute. Could you use a train or a railroad crossing sign to symbolize patience? (Or impatience?) Or the regularity of your morning routine? Do you choose spices from the pantry as you cook dinner? Could a small jar shape symbolize a flavorful life? Does your family like to go to the lake? Could a boat symbolize adventure or family or relaxation?

These examples may seem too specific. Or too general. Or too contrived. That's okay. They are just examples of ideas to consider as you explore the possibility of including symbols with personal meaning in your artwork.

Just Sitting, 44″ × 29″

Chairs are one of the personal symbols that appear in my art quilts. This chair invites you to sit and rest. You are surrounded by swirly possibilities of growth and adventure.

KEEP IT SIMPLE

It's helpful to look for symbols that can be translated into shapes that can be easily cut from fabric. For instance, it would be easier to cut out a music note than a saxophone.

Look for Symbols in Art

Think about your favorite artist and the shapes or images that appear in his or her work. Maybe you've studied an artist and know the history and meanings inherent in a body of work. Maybe you have no idea what an artist intended, but you can make your own interpretations. Reflecting on a piece of art can generate ideas for symbols to include in your own work and about what they might mean to you.

Green Bowl Gathering, 18″ × 18″

Leaves and other botanical shapes in the fabric and quilting motifs surround the bowl in this quilt. A tiny blossom peeks over the lip of the bowl. While creating this quilt, I thought about what I need in my life in order to grow and flourish. What do I need to fill up this bowl?

beautiful bowls

Bowls are a popular subject in mixed media art. I have a whole Pinterest board dedicated to artwork with bowls. To me, a bowl symbolizes simple nourishment. When I create a piece of art including a bowl, I think about the simplest things I need to feel nourished.

Possible Personal Symbols

What symbols could you consider incorporating into your art? Here are a few ideas to get the wheels turning. (Even a wheel would make a compelling symbol.) Maybe one of the things on this list will make you think of something else that may generate even more possibilities.

Possible Significance

What do all these items symbolize? They can mean whatever you want them to mean! A heart typically symbolizes love, but it might also symbolize health and wellness. Or sickness and loss. Consider pairing these themes with various symbols.

ADDING YOUR SYMBOLS TO YOUR COLLAGE

A symbol can be a focal point in your fabric collage or it can be a small detail. Think of a symbol as a shape that can be incorporated into any of the Eight Design Guides (page 22). A tree can be a symbol and the focal element in an art quilt based on the Symmetrical Design Guide. Stars can be symbols used in the Dancing Grid Design Guide. The Modular Design Guide can accommodate both simple and complex shapes or symbols.

Getting Started

After you've selected a potential symbol (or several), start with a great simple shape. Try drawing your symbols or explore images online. Use search words such as "clip art" or "silhouette" for helpful images and outlines. Use these images for reference when creating your own symbols.

After you've finalized the shape of your symbol, it's helpful to scan it into a computer and make prints in different sizes to trace or use as patterns.

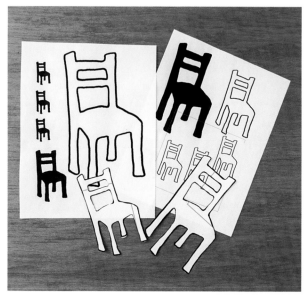

Patterns, printouts, and various other size options for a chair symbol

options and ideas

Keep in mind that all the techniques mentioned are simply ways to create shapes, patterns, and lines with fabric, paint, and stitching. You can use them to incorporate a symbol into your art quilt, but they can also be used in other ways to add interest to your work. Obviously you can use a freezer-paper stencil to make a ladder or a bowl, but you can also use freezer-paper stencils to create any other kind of shape or pattern.

Incorporating the Symbol

If you are adding a personal symbol to an art quilt after you've begun the composition, refer to the Design Checklist (page 30) for ideas about placement, color, and size.

If you are in the planning stages of creating an art quilt, consider the Eight Design Guides and how a personal symbol can be incorporated into any of the compositions.

Using Fabric

POSITIVE AND NEGATIVE SHAPES

Cut a symbol from prefused fabric and add it to your composition. Try both positive and negative images of a symbol. When cutting a shape, carefully cut around just the outline and you'll be left with the cut-out shape plus the leftover negative image of the shape, which can be used as an interesting design element.

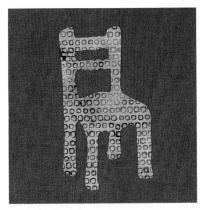

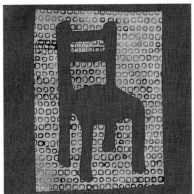

Positive and negative shapes

MIX IT UP

Try large and small versions of your symbol; consider mixing fabrics and sizes.

A mix of sizes and fabrics

NO PATTERNS

Simple shapes can be free-cut without any marking or pattern. You should definitely try this! It gives shapes character and personality.

Using Stitching

You can also use stitching to incorporate a shape or symbol on your art quilt. This can be done by machine or by hand.

HAND-EMBROIDERED OUTLINE

Cut out a pattern and mark it on your fabric using a blue disappearing-ink pen or chalk pencil. Use the backstitch to create a consistent detailed line. Choose embroidery floss or perle cotton and start stitching. Choose a color to blend or contrast. Either is fine. See Embroidery Stitches (page 68).

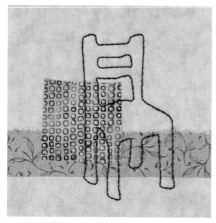

Symbol created with stitching

Mixing layers and materials is interesting. Think about placing the stitched outline in such a way that it overlaps various sections of the background of your collage. It's an opportunity to visually tie together different fabrics.

CLUSTERED STITCHES

Another option for creating a shape or symbol with hand embroidery is to stitch densely around the shape using straight stitches to create a negative image.

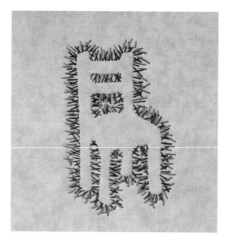

Dense stitches create a negative image.

MACHINE STITCHING

You can also outline the shape or symbol using free-motion quilting. Make several passes with the needle to create a thicker line.

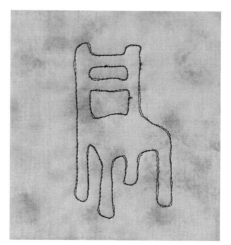

Use free-motion stitching to create an outline.

Adding a Personal Symbol and Other Details

The fabric background for your art quilt is fused. The fabric layer has potential for all kinds of additional details.

Remember, this Practice Exercise isn't a pattern! Follow along with the steps and images and recreate your own similar art quilt. Feel free to mix in your own designs, symbols, and ideas. Or create something entirely different, original, and unique.

1. Review the Design Checklist (page 30), paying attention to the questions in the Balance, Harmony, and Repetition sections. Where could you add a personal symbol? What size and color will it be?

2. Examine your fused composition. If you are using the example in the book, notice the following:

The white color from the focus fabric could be repeated in another area of the quilt.

The top half of the quilt could use more detail.

The tree is a large dark area.

3. Pick a symbol that is interesting to you and works with your art quilt.

> *The crescent moon is an interesting shape that blends with the rest of the design.*

> *This house feels a little too whimsical.*

> *This bird shape may be too detailed and may not contrast enough with the background fabric.*

> *This flower shape is too similar to the tree—just another irregular, circular botanical element.*

Possible symbols for the Practice Exercise are placed over the tree near the top of the quilt, since that area was identified as a potential design area. A white-on-white print balances the very dark colors in the rest of the quilt and picks up the light color in the focus fabric.

4. Create a pattern in the appropriate size to fit your collage.

5. Choose a technique for your symbol; see Adding Your Symbols to Your Collage (page 44).

6. Fuse or stitch the symbol onto your art quilt.

7. Referring again to the Design Checklist, consider whether you'd like to add more fabric details to your art quilt. Be sensitive to areas that feel like they need a little something. Be careful not to overdo it. Often less is more. Remember, you'll add paint and stitching layers later.

8. Fuse additional fabric details into place.

> *In the example here, I added a third leaf to one of the teal stalks to break the symmetry a bit.*

The crescent moon and the asymmetrical third leaf finish the fabric layer of this art quilt.

Explore possible personal symbols and potential meaning.

1. Draw a small circle in the center of a page in a sketchbook or on a piece of printer paper (or even the back of an envelope).

2. Divide the rest of the page into quarters. Label the sections "Significance," "Sketch," "Story," and "Similar."

3. Write the name of a possible symbol in the circle. Consider ideas from the possible personal symbols list (page 44).

4. Fill in each section as follows.

- Significance: Make a list of possible meanings for this symbol. Nothing is too obvious or too far-fetched. One idea may lead to another and another. Make note of anything that enters your mind. Consider what themes the symbol could suggest.

- Sketch: Draw a simple outline of the symbol. Sketch a few variations. (If you want more ideas, try a Google image search.)

- Story: Write a few lines about your personal connection to this image. What event does it remind you of? What feelings does it evoke? This is where you may surprise yourself with memories or ideas that don't seem related to the symbol. Be open to those unexpected connections.

- Similar: List or sketch other possible symbols related to these ideas.

Ask Yourself

- Do you like the idea of adding personal symbols to your work? (It's okay if you don't. You may be more drawn to using interesting shapes that don't need further meaning.)

- What surprised you about this exercise?

- Which section was the easiest to fill in?

- Which section felt difficult? Or complicated? Or useless?

- How might you use this symbol in your artwork?

- What other symbols could you explore with this exercise?

surface design

When Aqua Shines
10″ × 10″

The surface-design elements in this art quilt were carefully blended with all the other elements: purple circles were stamped with the rim of a jar, several of the circles were filled with blocks of handwriting, and the subtle tree shape with the wavy branches and buds was created using a freezer-paper stencil.

in this chapter

✱ Have fun with paint and ink.

✱ Think about creating a stash of fabric with original surface designs.

✱ Learn ways to add a layer of surface design to in-progress art quilts.

✱ Explore handwriting as a graphic element.

✱ Make prints with bubble wrap, sequin waste, and toilet paper tubes.

✱ Consider adding surface design to your Practice Exercise.

✱ Create a set of prints with found objects in the See What Happens exercise.

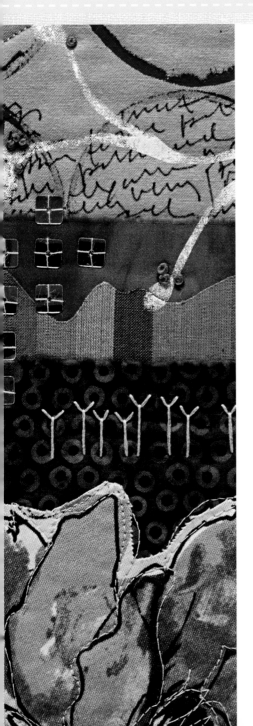

I create art quilts by building up layers of design. I try to make each layer interesting in its own way, but ultimately the layers need to work together and complement each other.

As I found my way into art quilting, I heard lots of artists talk about textile paints and dyes. Usually they were concerned with the "hand" of the fabric, meaning that they wanted the fabric to feel soft and drapey no matter how it was painted or dyed. Keeping the fabric soft and pliable is important if you're planning to wrap up in your quilt, but for small art quilts it doesn't make a big difference. In fact, I like the additional stiffness that paint can add to fabric. With this in mind, I use acrylic paint straight out of the tube.

WHAT IS SURFACE DESIGN?

Surface design is simply adding a layer of design to an existing fabric—it can be painted, stamped, stenciled, or printed, or you can use any other technique that adds to the surface. Start with plain white fabric or a solid fabric, or enhance a printed fabric with your original designs. There are several methods that offer many possibilities for enhancing your work.

All the methods included in this book are very accessible. They are easy techniques that use readily available and inexpensive supplies to create uncomplicated patterns with lots of potential.

The best thing about adding surface design to fabric is that you're adding unique marks. A commercial print can be used in many ways, but fabric with original surface design can only be created by you. Another wonderful benefit is the ability to create a pattern or color that fits the precise needs of any project at any time.

GET MESSY

I love paint as an additional layer in an art quilt. It introduces a new texture, reflecting light in different ways. Add it thick and globby like it's shouting or so faint that it's transparent and whispering.

BUILDING A STASH OF SURFACE-DESIGNED FABRICS

You can easily spend a day printing, stenciling, and stamping different fabrics in various colors with no specific quilt in mind in order to build a stash of fabric with a variety of surface designs to be used in future quilts.

Stash of surface-designed fabric

Various items used for stamping

CREATING SURFACE DESIGN FOR A SPECIFIC PROJECT

As you compose an art quilt, you can prepare surface-designed fabrics in colors and patterns that complement your palette, creating fabric for that specific project. Then you can fuse, cut, and incorporate it with other fabrics in the initial design stage.

ADDING SURFACE DESIGN TO AN IN-PROCESS COMPOSITION

You can also add surface design to an art quilt already in progress. Paint can complement a composition and tie together various elements. This can feel risky because the art quilt is already in progress, and once you add paint it's there to stay.

REASONS TO USE SURFACE DESIGN

How do you decide where, when, and how much to add? This is a great time to refer back to the Design Checklist (page 30). As you look over the questions in the Balance, Harmony, and Repetition sections, think about areas that could be improved and whether the solution might include a bit of surface design. Below are some options to consider.

Bring Out Colors

Adding a painted pattern that coordinates with the colors in your art quilt is a great way to visually connect all the elements.

Fill Spaces

If there is an area of your composition that feels empty, fill it with a bit of surface design. If the space just needs a little something, consider adding surface design in the same color as the background fabric. This will create a tone-on-tone design that will add interest but not detract from the other elements.

Add Variety of Texture

Paint sits on the surface of the cloth and adds a tiny bit of texture and dimension. Adding paint to fabric brings the artwork into the world of mixed media. Paint and fabric complement each other beautifully.

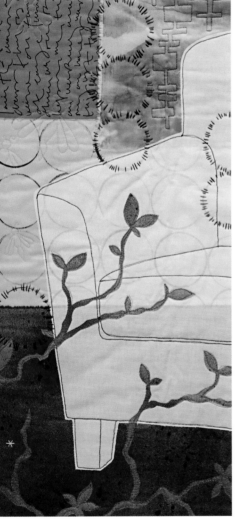

Just Sitting (page 43)

In this detail from *Just Sitting*, there are several examples of surface design: At the top is just a bit of handwriting on a solid blue fabric. The purple circles were stamped on the yellow fabric with the rim of a jar. The branch was created in two ways—I sprayed ink over a freezer-paper stencil to create the negative image; then I cut the branch out of another piece of fabric that had been sprayed with the same ink to fuse on top of the chair.

SURFACE DESIGN TECHNIQUES

I've been creating art quilts for years, and I use only acrylic paint and ink pens for all the surface design I add to my work. These media are readily available and make surface design easy, straightforward, and economical.

Below are simple techniques for adding surface design. Any of these can be used to create a stash of original fabric or added to an in-progress art quilt.

Paint

FOAM STAMPS

Use sticky-back fun foam to create an original stamp of your symbol. Draw (or trace) the symbol onto the foam, cut it out, and glue it onto a scrap of wood or a piece of Styrofoam cut from a recycled meat tray. You can also buy precut clear acrylic blocks designed for mounting stamps.

Using a foam stencil brush, add paint to the stamp and press it onto fabric. See how many impressions you can get before adding more paint. This creates an interesting pattern of lighter and darker images. When creating a stamp, remember to reverse the image if necessary.

Make your own stamps.

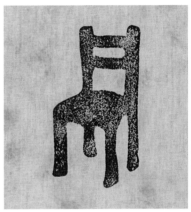

Stamped design

FREEZER-PAPER STENCILS

Freezer paper makes a great stencil to use with fabric. Draw (or trace) a shape or design onto the paper side of a piece of freezer paper. Use a craft knife to carefully cut out the shape.

Cut shapes from freezer paper.

Using an iron, press the freezer paper onto the surface of a piece of fabric or directly onto an in-progress art quilt. The waxy side will adhere to the fabric.

Dip a foam stencil brush in paint and blot off most of the paint. Starting at an edge of the stencil, begin filling in the shape with paint. If you're working on an in-progress art quilt, this part always feels risky. Be brave! Just plan carefully and don't use too much paint at first. It's easy to add more paint to make the symbol darker and more defined. If you need to, you can cover over anything you don't like with another layer of fabric.

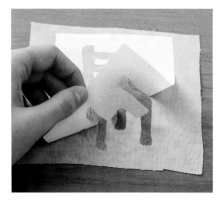

Stenciled image

OVER AND OVER!

A freezer-paper stencil can be used a few times, depending on how much paint builds up on the freezer paper and how long the wax still makes a good seal. When the freezer paper gets stiff and crinkly, it's time to trash the stencil.

Freezer-paper stencils can also be used to create positive and negative images.

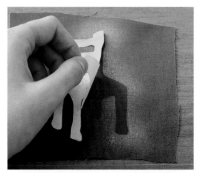

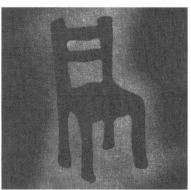

Negative version of the stencil

You don't have to fill in the whole stencil. You may wish to dab paint just around the edges so the shape is clear but slightly unfinished.

Partially stenciled images can be very evocative and effective.

She Sits to Create #12, 6″ × 6″

The dark blue twig-shaped tree was created with a freezer-paper stencil. I designed the stencil specifically to cross over the chair and onto the background fabric.

STAMPED PATTERNS WITH FOUND OBJECTS

Many items can be used as stamps. A mason jar makes an awesome tool for stamping circles on fabric. Commercial rubber stamps also work well. Create an original stamp with sticky-back fun foam using the method described in Foam Stamps (page 53). Other found objects make fabulous patterns; you're limited only by your imagination. Apply paint to a stamp by dipping the stamp directly into the paint spread on a palette. Or pick up paint on a foam stencil brush and then dab the paint onto the stamp. Stamp in a grid to create a simple, regular overall pattern, or stamp randomly.

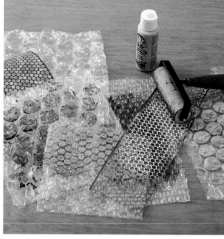

Bubble wrap and sequin waste supplies

Bubble Wrap

Bubble wrap makes great prints. You get the circles, but you also get the crinkly lines of the plastic. Large or small bubble wrap works fine. The bubbles can be popped or not; experiment to test the different results. It's easiest to add paint to bubble wrap using a brayer. Because you can see through the bubble wrap, you can control where the paint goes.

1. Roll out a thin layer of paint with a brayer.

2. Roll the paint onto the bubble wrap. Work quickly because acrylic paint dries relatively fast.

3. Press the painted side of the bubble wrap onto the cloth. Press firmly or lightly to get a strong or weak print.

4. To reuse the bubble wrap, rinse it or wipe it down.

Sequin Waste

Sequin waste can often be found in the ribbon section at craft stores. It's about 3″ wide and full of holes—it's the leftover material from the process of creating sequins. Sometimes it's called *punchinella*, and it makes a fabulous stencil.

1. Cut a 4″–5″ piece of sequin waste. This is an easy size to manipulate as you add paint.

2. With a foam stencil brush, pick up paint and blot most of the paint off to avoid wet, mushy prints. (Unless that's the look you're going for.)

3. Place the sequin waste over the section of cloth you want to print and begin dabbing paint through the holes.

4. Move the sequin waste around the fabric (or the in-progress art quilt) to add more pattern.

5. For a fun additional pattern, flip the sequin waste over and press it onto the cloth for a reverse print using the paint that has built up on the top side of the sequin waste.

Large and small bubble-wrap prints

Small bubble   Large bubble

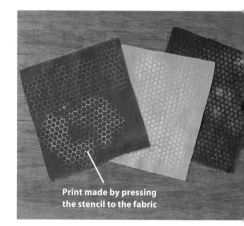

Print made by pressing the stencil to the fabric

Notice that the sequin waste was used as both a stencil and a print by flipping the painted stencil over and pressing it to the fabric.

Toilet Paper Roll Prints

You can print simple circles using an empty toilet paper roll, but you can also print many other shapes! Squeeze, fold, and manipulate the roll into an interesting shape. Dip it in paint and start printing. If you are creating a grid, rotate the tube with each print so there is a little variety within the pattern. Consider mixing colors for a two-tone effect. Or make several impressions with one color and then add a new color.

Toilet paper roll stamps

TRY IT OUT

Test paint colors and consistency on a scrap of fabric before printing on your quilt. Try out stamps, pens, and other techniques to master the design before moving on to your quilt.

A BIT OF CUSHION

With some objects, you may want to experiment with using a layer of felt under the fabric. A layer of felt gives the stamp something to sink into, and you may get a better print. Printing on a hard surface will produce different results.

Ink

HANDWRITING

Handwriting creates a loopy, graceful, irregular pattern. It can suggest communication, story, narrative, or journaling. Handwriting is completely personal—both the look of it and the content of it. Consider making the handwriting intentionally unreadable. Viewers will know that words and ideas are part of the art quilt, but let them imagine what the meanings might be.

Fabric with handwriting

Key Steps for Adding Handwriting to Fabric

1. Solid fabrics work best so the handwriting stands out clearly.

2. Iron the fabric to a sheet of freezer paper for stabilization as you write. (This is not absolutely necessary, but it's helpful. Feel free to try an unstabilized fabric and see how it works.)

3. Use a pen designed to be permanent on fabric, such as a Pigma Micron pen.

4. Just start writing.

5. Think of words in your mind, but stretch them out as you write. When your brain is moving faster than your hand, just skip words and keep writing. Thinking of words as you go will help you make specific letter forms rather than just bumps and loops.

6. Exaggerate long tails and loops as in the letter *y*. Make long dramatic lines as you cross your *t*'s and *f*'s.

Designing on Fabric or on In-Progress Quilts

Handwriting can be added to pieces of fabric to create a stash of surfaced-designed fabric, or it can be added to in-progress quilts. It can break up a space nicely, add a bit of interest, and symbolize themes explored in the quilt.

UNEXPECTED IDEAS

When I'm writing on fabric, I usually think and write about the symbols, ideas, and themes I'm exploring with the quilt. I use a stream-of-consciousness writing technique. If I'm making a quilt that includes houses, I may write and think about the different houses I've lived in: the places I liked living and the places I didn't enjoy, the people I met, the things I miss, or the places I hope to live in the future. Sometimes thoughts arise that I didn't expect. This can open new possibilities for inspiration and exploration.

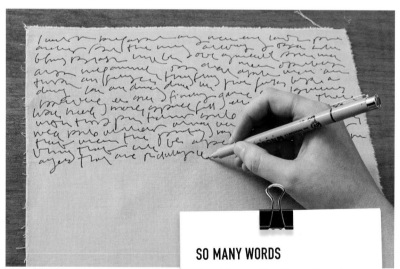

SO MANY WORDS

Consider stacking lines of handwriting close together for a tight, complex pattern. Alternatively, write loosely with lots of space between letters, words, and lines for a more airy feel.

practice exercise, part 3

Adding Surface Design

At the end of Part 2 (page 47), you completed the fabric layer of design and added a personal symbol using fabric, paint, or stitching. Now you can consider your options for adding painted patterns, stamps, or handwriting.

You'll see various options with this Practice Exercise, but feel free to choose your own patterns, designs, and colors.

1. Review the Design Checklist (page 30), thinking carefully about Balance, Harmony, and Repetition. How can a bit of surface design enhance your composition?

2. Take a look at your quilt-in-progress. If you are using the example from the book, consider the following:

✳ The white color of the moon can be repeated.

✳ Small details can balance out the large, simple shapes in the rest of the composition.

✳ The tree and teal leafy stalks can be tied in to the rest of the composition.

> In my sample, I used a mason jar and white paint to stamp circles on the quilt, lightly overlapping the tree and the teal leafy stalks. Then I added two lines of handwriting following the shape of the hillside.

3. Consider the other surface design possibilities in this chapter.

4. Be brave! Add some surface design to your art quilt.

The white circles repeat the color of the moon. They also visually tie the tree and leafy stalks to the rest of the quilt because they overlap those shapes. The lines of handwriting along the hillside are subtle but offer an interesting detail to viewers who look closely at the art quilt.

Try creating patterns based on a simple grid rather than a random allover pattern. Within the grid format, you can experiment with different colors and amounts of paint. Printing fabric is the kind of technique that you really need to try to truly get a feel for the potential and the process.

1. Cut 4 pieces 6″ × 6″ of a solid-color fabric. Place the fabric on top of a piece of felt. The felt will allow the stamps to sink into the fabric a bit and make good prints.

2. Choose a paint color that coordinates with your fabric color.

3. Find 4 objects that might make an interesting print. Consider Legos or other items from the toy box, a spool of thread, sponges, a fork, items from nature, small plastic boxes, or kitchen tools. (Choose smallish objects that will fit on the 6″ × 6″ fabric.)

4. Squeeze some paint onto a foam tray or other palette.

5. Apply paint to the object with a foam stencil brush or dip the stamp directly into the paint.

6. Stamp or print onto a square of fabric with the object. Start in a corner and fill the square with a regular repeated pattern.

7. Stamp or print again before adding more paint to the stamp. This will create some dark and light impressions.

8. Repeat the process with each of the found objects and the other squares of fabric.

I used a small binder clip, an empty thread spool, a square Lego, and a plastic toy tree trunk as stamps for this exercise.

These simple repeat patterns have great potential to be cut up and combined with other fabrics for art quilts. Notice that some of the prints are dark and some light, depending on whether the stamp had fresh paint or was on the second or third impression.

GET A GRIP

When printing with found objects such as spools or small toys, it's best to choose an item that has a built-in handle. A spool works great because you can hold it easily and control the placement of the print. A coin would be difficult to print with because it's so flat.

EXPLORE FURTHER

After trying some of these simple surface-design techniques, you may want to explore others. There are lots of great books, classes, and online tutorials … so many possibilities.

ASK YOURSELF

- Do you like the regular grid? Or do you wish it were more random?

- Did you find the repetitive process boring? Or meditative?

- Did any of the objects create an unexpected design?

- Could you rotate the objects for different results?

- Did you make any mistakes? Are they really mistakes?

- What other objects might make interesting prints?

- Did you choose a paint color with high contrast to the fabric? How would the pattern be different if you chose a paint that blended with the fabric?

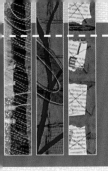

stitching

Glimpse, 60″ × 24″

Stitching takes many forms in this quilt. There are subtle areas of linear free-motion stitching in the gray background. Shiny, variegated thread in yellow, orange, and red suggests waving wheat in the area beneath the windmill. Stitched X's secure folded-up bits of magazine pages to the surface of the quilt. An irregular hand-embroidered blanket stitch creates partial circles at the edges of the quilt.

in this chapter

✳ Learn when, where, and how to add machine and hand stitching to your art quilts.

✳ Discover the possibilities of creating and using a stitch map when planning the stitched layer of your art quilt.

✳ Consider hand embroidery for outlines, filler, and trailing designs.

✳ Consider machine stitching for gentle curves, straight lines, sketchy outlines, and free-motion motifs.

✳ Try a few favorite embroidery stitches.

✳ Plan and add stitching to your Practice Exercise.

✳ Explore the meditative quality of hand embroidery in the See What Happens exercise.

The stitching is what makes a quilt a quilt. For me, it's the very best part of working as a fiber artist. If painters love the look of every brushstroke, I love the look of every stitch. Stitching also has the amazing beauty of being part of the construction and part of the design. With traditional quilts and art quilts, the stitching holds together the three layers of cloth. It can also add color, pattern, and texture. I love creating interesting motifs with free-motion stitching. Hand embroidery creates a personal, unique layer of design in an art quilt. Viewers sense the intimate process of stitching. I certainly feel the personal connection after pulling miles of floss through the cloth and spending hours with the quilt sitting in my lap.

STITCHING FOR ART QUILT COLLAGES

With fused art quilt collages, technically no stitching is required to hold everything together. Sometimes stitching goes through all three layers; sometimes it's decorative and just goes through the top and batting or felt. Sometimes it's done by machine and sometimes by hand. It's always an important design element and an opportunity to add interest.

For hand embroidery, it's usually easier to stitch through the top layer and the batting only. These two layers are flexible and easy to handle but have enough body to stitch without an embroidery hoop. Because the backing will be added later, you don't have to worry about keeping the stitches on the back neat. The same is true of machine stitching. You can always add more stitching through all three layers if you choose.

Green Bowl Gathering
(page 43)

Machine stitching adds another layer of design to this quilt. The bowl and the flower in the bowl are outlined with free-motion quilting. There are several botanical shapes stitched in the background with a matching thread color. They add interest but don't detract from the fabric elements. There are also several blocks of stitched, stacked straight lines that visually connect different elements on the quilt.

MACHINE STITCHING—FEED DOGS UP

Enjoy the process of stitching layers of fabric together by running them under the needle of your home sewing machine. There is endless potential to create lines, patterns, and imagery with stitching. It can also add dimension, texture, and color to beautifully complement the fabric layer.

Straight-Line Quilting

Straight-line quilting uses the feed dogs and a regular sewing machine foot. The machine guides the fabric under the needle at a regular pace. Even though it's called straight-line quilting, you can make gentle (and some not-so-gentle) curves with this method. You can also stop stitching and pivot the quilt around the needle to change directions. This will create corners or angled stitching lines.

Straight-Stitched Outline

Outline a shape with a single straight line. This line of stitching was created with the feed dogs up using a regular foot. The fabric was pivoted at each corner, making for a precise, straight line. You can also echo quilt by stitching several rows around the shape, like concentric circles. A machine-stitched line is thin and delicate. Consider stitching over the same line a few times to give it more emphasis.

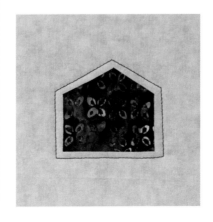

Machine-Stitched Curves

Add details with lines of gentle curves. The arch over the house was stitched with the feed dogs up using a regular foot by slowly turning the fabric to create the curve. Overlapping lines add interest and suggest movement.

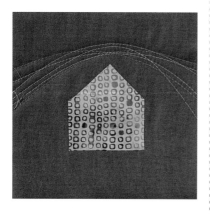

Simple Lines

If an area calls out to be filled with stitches but not necessarily a motif or design, simple lines are a great option.

FREE-MOTION QUILTING—FEED DOGS DOWN

With free-motion quilting on a home sewing machine, the feed dogs are dropped and you guide the fabric under the needle in any direction to create a line.

Free-Motion Sketchy Outline

Stitch a sketchy outline of a shape by dropping the feed dogs and stitching an irregular repeated outline. This blends the edges of the fabric and suggests a hand-drawn line. Several passes around the house shape allow the lines to overlap for more expressive details. Notice the difference between the straight-stitched outline (page 63) and the free-motion sketchy outline.

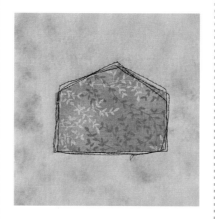

Free-Motion Motifs

Add a free-motion quilted motif. Here, flowers and leafy ferns are stitched using free-motion quilting. The house shape almost frames the whimsically stitched lines.

Free-Motion Quilted Background

Fill the background with free-motion quilting to allow other fabric shapes to pop. These swirls and zigzags add interest to the background. Because the house has no quilting, it stands out a bit with the loft of the batting.

Grass and Flowers

Botanical motifs are fun to create using free-motion stitching. These kinds of images lend themselves nicely to a long horizontal strip of quilting that can cross over different fabrics and sections of an art quilt.

Echoed Patterns in the Fabric

Patterns and motifs from the fabrics in a quilt can be repeated with free-motion stitching. The stitching can follow the actual lines in the fabric, or the motifs can be copied and repeated in other areas of the art quilt.

Haze and Hope (page 21)

A free-motion quilted line of ferns, grasses, and flowers fills the purple strip of fabric above the pebbles. It's unrefined and rather subtle, but it adds an interesting layer of design.

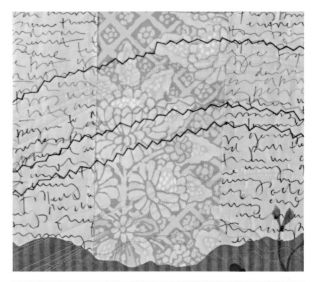

DON'T GIVE UP

The single most important tip for mastering free-motion quilting is simply practice.

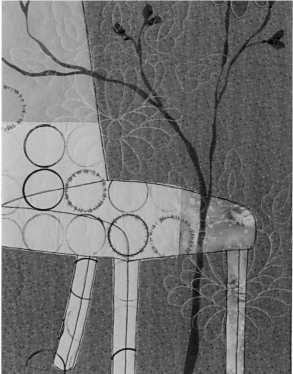

Blue Chair Mantra (page 14)

I loved the pattern in the yellow fabric in the sky section of this quilt. I copied the shape and repeated it with free-motion quilting in the lower right-hand section.

HAND STITCHING

Hand stitching is very different from machine stitching, but you'll love it for some of the same reasons. Rather than pushing the fabric under the needle of the machine, you pull the needle through the layers of fabric. There is a little snap as the eye of the needle tugs the floss through the layers. It's so satisfying! The repetitive motion of creating each individual stitch is meditative and relaxing.

Hand embroidery infuses the mark of the artist into the quilt. Each stitch is deliberately placed within the design by the process of pulling the needle through the fabric.

Embroidered Outlines

Add interest to any shape by outlining or framing it with hand embroidery. The house is outlined with several individual straight stitches in yellow, making it look a bit like the house is glowing. There is also a simple line of green stitching just inside the edge of the fabric house shape.

Overlapped Outlines

Repeat a motif by stitching the shape and overlapping other fabrics. Outlining a small green house and a large purple house creates a little neighborhood when the houses are layered over the white fabric.

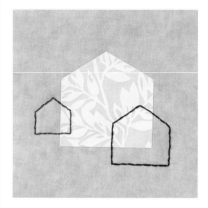

Framed Fabric Shapes

Use a running stitch to outline a shape. Below, the house is outlined with a contrasting color that draws interest to the shape. Notice that it's a bit irregular and wonky. That makes it interesting. A purple asterisk is stitched over one of the polka dots. Use the pattern of a printed fabric as inspiration for tiny embroidered details.

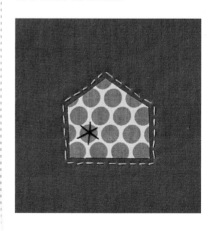

grandma's chair

I often hand stitch my art quilts while watching TV with my family. I sit in the same chair where my grandmother knit sweaters for my cousins and me. The low arms make it perfect for stitching. I can stretch my arms out as I pull the thread and not feel constrained. It's low to the ground, so I can easily reach all my supplies in my stitching basket.

Photo by Deborah Boschert

Filler Stitch

Cover a shape with a filler stitch. Here the seed stitch fills the house shape.

Overlapped Embroidered Motifs

Trail stitches over and across a fabric shape. These teal Y stitches run from the green background fabric over the purple house and back to the background. This makes a visual connection between the foreground and background.

Swarm

Create a swarm of stitching over an area of an art quilt. These light blue cross-stitches seem to float over the house and can lead the eye from one area of the quilt to another.

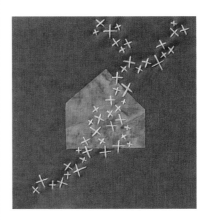

Haze and Hope (page 21)

There are several hand-stitched motifs across the design of this quilt. Irregular stacked cross-stitches contrast with the swirly green vines stitched over the house. Blue asterisks warm across the house and up through the trees.

Embroidery Stitches

BACKSTITCH

This stitch makes a beautiful solid line and can outline complex shapes. Detail can be achieved by taking smaller stitches around curves and points. For specific shapes, it's best to mark the stitching line ahead of time. Use a water-soluble blue pen or a chalk pencil, depending on which shows up better on the fabric.

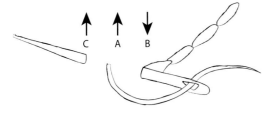

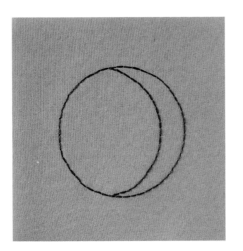

Y STITCH

My favorite stitch! It's a simple stitch that can suggest wildflowers or trees.

Stitch the vertical lines first. This allows you to align the stitches so they are all parallel. (Or angle them so they look wilder.) You can also decide how close together you want each Y. Take a second pass with the thread across the quilt, adding the Y angle on top of each stem. The Y stitch works best with several clustered together in a line.

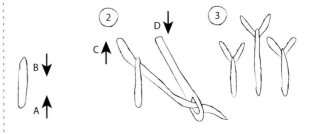

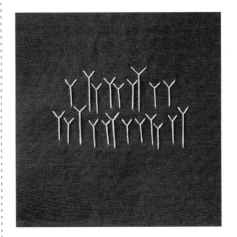

IRREGULAR BAR

Stack several stitches together in a line. They can be slightly different lengths and distributed at slightly different intervals. (That's the irregular part.) This combination of stitches makes a big impact because it looks like a thick bar of color even though it's made of individual stitches. (That's the bar part.)

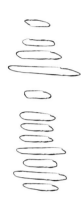
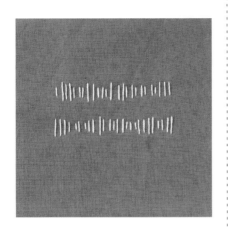

SEED STITCH

The seed stitch is great as a filler stitch, but it can also be used to trail across the art quilt like seeds blowing in the wind. Stitches are clustered together at different angles. They can be tightly or loosely spaced and can be long or short stitches. Stitches can be consistent in spacing and length within a space—or not, creating an entirely different look.

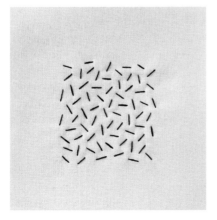

CROSS-STITCH

There are many ways to use the classic cross-stitch. Cross-stitches can be stacked in a regular arrangement to create a block of stitches. As with the seed stitch, they can be placed more randomly to trail across an area or to fill a space. It's fun to mix small and large crosses. The angle of the cross can vary to create anything from a plus sign to a multiplication symbol.

For a slight variation, stitch an asterisk. It's just like a cross-stitch, but it has three lines rather than just two.

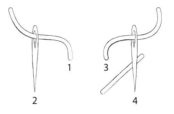

STITCHING POSSIBILITIES

Any of the stitching ideas and techniques presented in this chapter can be used in a variety of ways. Think about how they can be repeated, extended, enlarged, or modified and used on a larger quilt.

PLANNING AND DESIGNING THE STITCHING LAYER

The fabric composition is complete, the paint is dry, and everything is fused to felt or batting. It's time to plan the last layer of design: the stitching. Using the ideas in this chapter, you are ready to take this on.

Take a Reference Photo

Start by taking a picture of the in-progress art quilt. Try to avoid heavy shadows and get a straight-on image, but a simple snapshot is fine. On your computer, crop the image as if you were finishing the edges of the art quilt. It's helpful to remove the visual distraction of the unfinished edges and anything else in the photo. Print out three to five copies of the image on regular printer paper.

Make a Stitch Map

Sketch, doodle, and make notes on these printouts. If you doodle on three printouts and still have more ideas, print more sheets. This is a great way to audition possibilities, and you can really see how potential lines of stitching can complement the rest of the composition. Doodle possibilities for both machine and hand stitching.

You can refer to the Design Checklist (page 30) for ideas about where to fill in stitching, what colors to consider, and motifs to incorporate.

Eventually, settle on a plan and create a stitch map on one of the printouts. Include lines representing stitching in each of the different areas of the quilt. Create a key for yourself to indicate color, shape, and machine or hand embroidery.

Gather the appropriate embroidery floss and begin stitching. As you are stitching, you won't have to think about what color or what stitch belongs in what area because you have already planned it out. Simply focus on the task of stitching, without stopping to make design decisions.

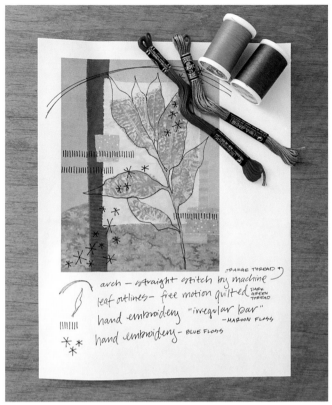

The stitch map for *Autumn Advances* includes notes to follow for each section of stitching.

Autumn Advances, 10½″ × 8½″

Hand and Machine Stitching

Your art quilt is coming along! The fabric is fused to the felt batting. Details and symbols have been added, and a bit of surface design complements the whole composition. Now it's time to add a layer of stitching.

1. Take a picture of the in-progress art quilt. Try to take it straight on so the shape is not distorted by the angle of the camera.

2. Looking at your Practice Exercise at this stage, think about possible areas for improvement or enhancement. In the example quilt, consider the following:

3. Print out several images of the quilt on regular printer paper. Make the image of the quilt fill up about ¾ of the page. Use the space around the image to doodle and make notes. Sketch possible stitch designs on the printouts.

4. Finalize the plans for the stitching. Choose thread, floss, and perle cotton colors and make a key on the stitching map to match stitches with colors.

5. Complete your machine stitching.

6. Add hand embroidery.

The white circles may stand out too much.

The moon feels a bit like it's floating.

The tree is still a big open space.

More small details would add interest.

7. Gently press the quilt, taking care not to flatten any dimensional stitching.

The light aqua stitching over some of the white circles adds detail and slightly tones down the brightness of the paint. The Y stitches and French knots in the tree add detail and suggest a kind of magical realism in this unique landscape; they also break the symmetry of the composition for added interest. Free-motion stitching around the edges of the leafy stalks, the blue tree, and the moon visually connects all the shapes together. The machine-stitched arches at the top of the quilt fill the space and direct the eye down to the center of the quilt.

This exercise will give you a feel for the meditative, relaxing, creative process of stitching by hand. You'll also see the potential of clustering several stitches together.

1. Cut a 6″ × 6″ square of prefused fabric. A solid color or something that reads solid is best. Fuse it to a 6″ × 6″ piece of felt.

2. Gather some embroidery floss that looks great with the fabric. Up to 3 colors will be good; use whatever you like. Maybe contrast is interesting to you, maybe you like the idea of tone-on-tone, or maybe you want a little of both.

3. Choose one of the stitches included in Embroidery Stitches (page 68). Or choose another stitch you're eager to explore.

4. Using 3 strands of floss, begin stitching in the middle of the fabric/felt square. Starting in the middle gives you the rest of the fabric to hold on to, and the fabric won't get as distorted as it would if you started in a corner.

5. Begin filling the entire square with your chosen stitch.

6. Explore placing stitches close together and farther apart.

7. Switch colors of floss when you run out, or whenever you feel like it.

8. Fill the entire square with stitches; then press lightly to smooth and flatten.

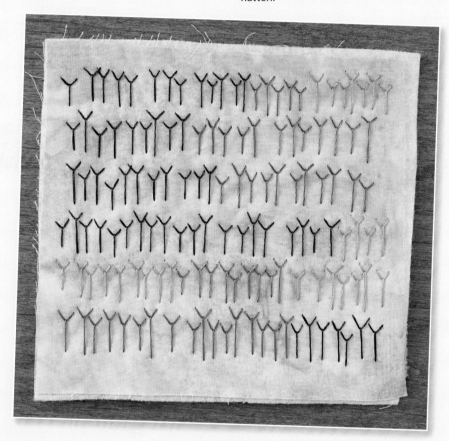

ASK YOURSELF

- Did you find the process meditative? Monotonous? Boring? Challenging? Relaxing? Creative?

- Did you want to try a different stitch? Or were you engaged with just one stitch?

- Was there anything you found surprisingly challenging about the project? Anything too simple?

- How could you make it more or less challenging?

- How do you feel about your color choices now that the exercise is complete?

- How would different stitches create different results?

- Did your tools work for you? The needle? The thimble? The size of the cloth?

finishing

Wider Possibilities
12″ × 10″

This quilt was inspired by a quote from Pearl Bailey: "Never, never rest contented with any circle of ideas, but always be certain that a wider one is still possible." Thinking about the idea of circles, I chose two different polka-dot fabrics and printed more circles with a foam dart and jar. The chair alludes to the idea of resting but is surrounded by color and pattern and movement and possibilities.

in this chapter

- ✳ Learn how to fuse the backing and square up your art quilt.

- ✳ Make note of several tips for measuring and cropping.

- ✳ Consider various edge treatments, including fused binding, zigzag stitching, and painted edges.

- ✳ Review options for displaying your art quilt.

- ✳ Learn how to mount a small quilt on a wrapped canvas.

- ✳ Pick a title and create a label.

- ✳ Finish your Practice Exercise.

- ✳ Incorporate all you've learned and create a small art quilt using the parameters selected by rolling dice in the See What Happens exercise.

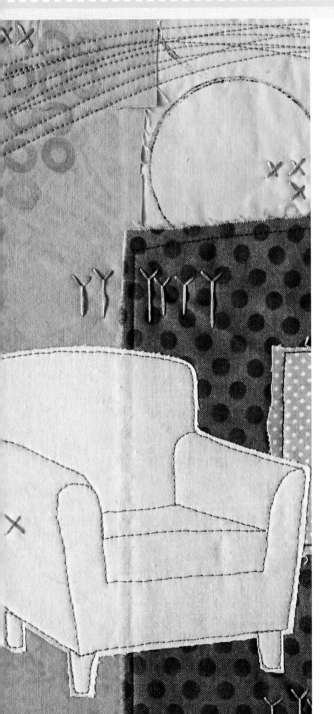

People often ask how to tell when an art quilt is finished. I'm always asking myself the same question. The answer is always different. Sometimes I'm delighted by the whole process: everything works and the final details are clear. Sometimes a deadline approaches and the quilt must be completed. Sometimes nothing feels quite right and I just abandon an in-progress piece. (Life's too short.) Sometimes I need a break from a particular project, so I set it aside for awhile. Sometimes I've enjoyed the whole process right up to finishing the edges, but ended with a piece that's not quite what I had hoped it would be. It's all part of the process.

Finishing a piece of art is so satisfying! I encourage you to embrace the whole process and work toward completion. Then start on your next art quilt!

PRESSING

The front of your art quilt is complete. All the fabric elements have been fused down to the batting or felt, surface design enhances the design, machine stitching has been added, and the hand embroidery is complete.

Using a hot iron, press the quilt one last time from both the front and the back to make sure it is flat from edge to edge—use a pressing cloth if you included paint or fragile materials such as tulle, polyester felt, or other synthetic fibers.

FINAL DESIGN REVIEW

Refer to the Edges and Fine-Tuning sections of the Design Checklist (pages 31 and 32). Even though you've made careful design decisions throughout the creative process, it's good to give the quilt one last look before finishing. (After fusing on the back and finishing the edges, it's much harder to make changes.)

FUSED BACKINGS

As long as you've fused the front of the quilt, you might as well fuse the backing.

1. Cut a piece of fabric for the backing of the quilt. Cut it slightly larger than the quilt to allow for cropping.

2. Press the backing fabric and prepare it with fusible web (see Working with Fusible Web, page 38).

3. Fuse the backing fabric to the back of the quilt.

SQUARING UP AND CROPPING

Most quilts will need cropping and squaring up at this point.

1. Place the quilt on a cutting mat. If the art quilt is small, all the measuring and cropping can be done on a cutting mat.

2. Using a ruler and rotary cutter, trim one side.

3. Using the marks on the cutting mat to make sure the 2 sides are parallel, trim the opposite side.

4. Using a ruler and the marks on the cutting mat, decide where the top will be cut.

5. Check the ruler and mat to make sure the corners are 90°.

6. Trim the top.

7. Again, use the markings on the mat to make sure the bottom is parallel and the corners are square. Then trim the bottom.

8. Press the quilt again to make sure the cut edges are all fully fused and the quilt is still flat.

Tips for Trimming, Cropping, and Measuring

- If there is a strong horizontal or vertical line in the design of your quilt, you can measure from that line to the parallel edges. This will ensure that the quilt doesn't appear tilted after it's squared up.

- If the design of your art quilt is symmetrical, consider measuring from the center of the quilt to each side. This will ensure that the shapes in the middle of the design are actually in the middle of the quilt.

- If you want to mount your quilt on canvas or in a frame, you may need to crop to a specific size. If so, use a measuring tape to mark exactly where you'll be cutting on each side.

- The key to trimming up large quilts is to place them on a large, flat surface. Then measure and remeasure from side to side, making sure the top and bottom and left and right sides are parallel. This means measuring at each end and in the middle of opposite sides to make sure all those measurements are the same. Use these measurements to mark cutting lines, and then cut with scissors or a rotary cutter.

- Quilts don't have to be rectangular or square. Experiment with wavy edges or angled corners.

- Keep the edges that were trimmed from the quilt when cropping. They make excellent practice pieces for auditioning different edge finishes.

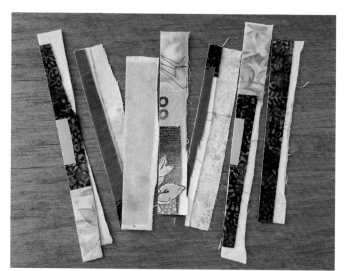

These edges were trimmed off the example quilts for the Eight Design Guides. They could be used to test paint colors for a painted edge, or they could be used to test edge treatments (next page) such as zigzagging or decorative stitches.

EDGE TREATMENTS

Now it's time to think about how to finish the edges.

Fused Binding

The fused binding is reminiscent of a traditional quilt binding. It's a piece of fabric that wraps around the edge of a quilt and shows on the front and the back. If an art quilt needs a visual border, this is a good opportunity to add a narrow strip of color or pattern that will complement the design of the quilt.

The lime green fabric was fused over the edge. A line of machine stitching secures the edge and complements the teal in this example.

1. Cut strips of prefused fabric approximately 1½˝ wide.

2. Place a sheet of Silicone Release Paper on the ironing surface.

3. Place the quilt faceup on the release paper.

4. Place the prefused strip of binding so that approximately ¼˝ is on the quilt and the rest of the strip is hanging off onto the release paper.

5. Using a hot iron, fuse the binding strip to the quilt. Ease and adjust the binding strip with the fingers of your left hand while holding the iron with your right. If you are left-handed, adjust with your right hand while holding the iron with your left.

6. If needed, add more strips to finish an edge. Overlap the strips by ⅛˝. It's okay if the strips go beyond the corner. They will be trimmed.

7. Let the strips cool.

8. Carefully lift the quilt, peeling the edges of the binding strips off the release paper.

9. At the corners, trim the binding strips flush with the edge of the art quilt.

10. Turn the quilt over and gently but firmly fold the binding strip around to the back of the quilt and fuse.

11. Repeat for the other sides.

12. Add a line of machine stitching on top of the fused binding, approximately ⅛˝ from the edge, if desired.

WHAT COLOR BINDING?

- You can use a contrasting-colored binding to frame the piece.

- You can use different fabrics: one fabric for the bottom of the quilt to ground it, and a different fabric for the other three sides.

- You can match the fabric to the body of the quilt. This creates the illusion of the design of the quilt extending all the way to the edge, rather than being framed with a binding. Plan ahead to make sure the colors line up.

This very simple quilt illustrates a matching fused binding. Notice that the binding fabric in the sky section is not the exact same as the sky in the quilt, but it is visually similar. You can add interest with fabric choices.

Painted Edge

A painted edge seals the fabric at the edges of the quilt, covers the white color of the felt or batting, and adds just a scant bit of color on the top of the quilt at the very edge—a halo of color. This technique works especially well with felt as the middle layer. Although batting spreads a bit at the edges even when dabbed with paint, it's still a great option to consider.

A painted edge

1. Choose a coordinating color of paint. Squirt some onto a palette.

2. Pick up a bit of paint on a foam stencil brush and then blot most of it off.

3. Carefully dab paint along the edges of the quilt. If the brush is too dry, add just a little more paint at a time.

4. Let each side dry before moving on to the next side.

Zigzag Edge

A simple zigzag stitch is another great option for finishing edges. Because the top and the back are fused to the batting, the art quilt has enough body to stay flat and stiff as the needle passes over. This is especially true if felt is used as the batting.

Practice on one of the trimmed-off edges of the quilt. Decide exactly what color thread to use and make note of the preferred length and width of the zigzag stitch. Any options from wide to narrow and tight to loose are fine.

When you reach the corner of the quilt, stop with the needle down in the quilt. Lift the presser foot and pivot the quilt. Put the presser foot back down and hand crank the needle off the edge of the quilt; carefully adjust the quilt as needed to ensure that the needle will return into the quilt aligned for stitching the edge. Then begin stitching on the next side.

Using one color of thread creates a clean, simple line.

Take another pass or two with different thread colors to create a layer of color and unexpected detail. With this technique, it's a good idea to slightly vary the stitch length with each color, so the stitches don't end up sitting right on top of the previous color.

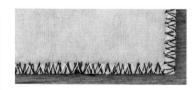

Using variegated thread creates a striped edge. To get the full effect, the stitches need to be quite close together. It's okay if some of the fabric still shows through. Use a coordinating solid-color thread in the bobbin.

keeping it small

I'll let you in on a little secret. When you focus on creating small art quilts, it's easier to get them done! Small works just don't take as much time as larger pieces. Small works are easier to manipulate and measure on a regular worktable. Small works are even easier to hang and display. I have made large art quilts, some as big as 50˝ × 50˝. These same ideas, techniques, and methods work with large quilts. It just takes a bit more time, planning, patience, and dedication. I encourage you to embrace the possibilities of working relatively small. Small art quilts in the range of 10˝–25˝ are a delight to create and finish.

TITLES

Now that your quilt is finished, give it a title! Anything goes. The title can be simple and obvious, like *Yellow Ladder* (page 41). Or it can reflect the theme, as with *Glimpse* (page 61). The following are some ideas to help you with your titles:

- Pick a few words from a song or poem.

- Try something with alliteration ("Rosy Red Raspberries").

- Choose a simple noun and a word to describe it: "Tall House," "Green Bowl," or "Early Garden."

- Try not to use predictable phrases such as "Tea for Two" or "Home Is Where the Heart Is." You created an original piece of art, so make your title original.

- Title the quilt after a place, even if the quilt doesn't specifically or obviously reference the location.

- Think about word variations such as "grow," "growing," "growth." My quilt *Drift and Detour* (page 26) could have been titled *Drifting and Detouring*, or just *Drift*. Or *Drifted*. Or just *Detour*. Each option sounds a little bit different and suggests a slightly different meaning.

- Use an online thesaurus—type in a word that describes something in your quilt, such as "house," "garden," or "polka dot." See if any of the words that come up could be worked into an interesting title.

LABELS

It's important to include a label. An easy way to label your work is to simply hand write the information on a piece of prefused fabric and iron it to the back of the quilt. Be sure to include your name and the title of the quilt at the very least. Think about adding the year you made it, where you live, and the dimensions of the quilt. If the quilt was made for a special occasion or as a gift, you may want to include that information on the label.

PRESENTATION

There are many options for hanging art quilts. The important thing is to get them on the wall and enjoy them!

Loops or Rings

Many art quilts are small enough to hang with simple loops sewn at the top two corners of the back of the quilt. You can find small plastic rings at most fabric stores. You can also use the metal pop-tops from cans of soda. These are great because they have two holes: one that can be sewn through to attach the tab to the back of the quilt and one that can slip onto a small nail for hanging. Small art quilts are lightweight. Often, two simple sewing pins carefully hammered into the wall are adequate for hanging. Plus, pins leave almost no hole in the wall.

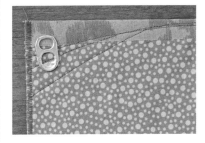

Sleeve

For a larger art quilt, a hanging sleeve sewn to the top of the quilt is the most common method of display. A dowel, wooden slat, or curtain rod slides through the sleeve. The dowel extends just past the ends of the sleeve and rests on two nails in the wall.

Mounting on Canvas

Mounting art quilts on stretched canvas is a great way to display your work. It gives the quilt presence and visibility when hanging on the wall. Stretched canvases are available at craft stores in a variety of sizes and depths. There are several ways to use stretched canvases.

EDGE-TO-EDGE MOUNTS

Art quilts can be mounted on canvases so that the quilt is the same size as the canvas and the edges of the quilt reach the edge of the canvas. This is a clean, contemporary presentation. If you are using this method, plan ahead to make the art quilt fit the specific size of the canvas. Also check to make sure canvas is available in the desired size.

Blue and Gold View #3, 8˝ × 8˝

1. Use a wrapped canvas the same size as the art quilt.

2. Using a coordinating color of acrylic paint, paint the canvas, covering the sides and the edges of the top. There is no need to paint the whole top of the canvas, as it will be covered by the art quilt.

3. Paint additional coats as needed.

4. Let it dry completely.

Supplies for mounting a small art quilt on a stretched canvas

5. Squeeze glue onto the surface of the canvas and spread it thinly over the whole canvas using an old credit card. Be sure to spread glue all the way to the edges. Use an all-purpose or tacky glue that is permanent when dry.

6. Carefully line up the quilt on the canvas. Scoot and adjust the quilt so it is aligned perfectly on the canvas.

7. Carefully smooth the quilt from edge to edge, using your hands.

8. Firmly press along all the edges, using your fingers, so the quilt catches glue all the way around.

9. Place the canvas on a hard surface. Cover the quilt with a clean cloth. Place several heavy books on top. Let dry overnight.

FLOATING MOUNTS

It's also possible to mount an art quilt of any size on a canvas that is slightly larger than the quilt. The quilt floats in the middle of the canvas, and the rest of the canvas acts as a mat to visually frame the quilt. Paint the entire canvas. Rather than glue, hand stitch the art quilt to the canvas when using the floating style. This offers the advantage of being able to remove the quilt from the canvas in the future if desired.

Finishing

It's almost done! At the end of Part 4 (page 71), you pressed the art quilt from both the front and back.

1. Choose a fabric for the backing. Cut the backing fabric approximately 1″ larger on all sides than the quilt top. Prepare the backing fabric with fusible web (see Fused Backings, page 75).

2. Fuse the backing fabric to the back of the quilt.

3. Trim your quilt (see Squaring Up and Cropping, page 76).

Trimming the edges

4. Finish the edges (see Edge Treatments, page 77).

5. Come up with an inspired title (see Titles, page 79).

6. Make a label and fuse it to the back (see Labels, page 79).

7. Hang your art quilt (see Presentation, page 79).

Dusk Begins in Blue, 16″ × 12″

I decided to use a strip of light aqua as a fused binding along the bottom edge. This repeats the aqua from the hand-stamped gray fabric beneath the tree trunk and the aqua rectangles on each side. I machine stitched around the other three edges, just a tiny ⅛″ from the edge. Then I dabbed the edges with light blue paint.

For added detail, I hand embroidered using an overcast stitch along the bottom edge, following the blue of the tree trunk and the teal of the leafy stalks.

Here's a challenge! Sometimes restrictions and specific parameters generate fabulous ideas. Now that you've explored creating layers of design with fabric, paint, and stitching, you're ready to continue creating your own original art quilts. See what ideas may arise with this exercise.

1. Grab a die. (You can probably find one in a board game box in the hall closet.)

2. Refer to the chart for the theme, color palette, and detail.

3. Roll the die for a theme to work with.

4. Roll again for a color palette.

5. Finally, roll once more for a detail to include.

6. Make note of the three requirements.

7. Begin brainstorming and making notes about ideas for a small art quilt with these parameters.

8. Feel free to reroll if you're annoyed by any of the options. No one's looking. Reroll until you're inspired or willing to take on the challenge.

9. Think about which of the Eight Design Guides might work for the options you rolled. Make some sketches. Pick out some fabric.

10. Create a small art quilt! Maybe it's possible that just brainstorming and sketching will get the creative juices flowing. Maybe you'll want to make this quilt. Maybe you'll be motivated to make something else entirely.

Storm Clouds, 7½˝ × 8˝

With my die, I rolled a 4, 3, and 4, which gave me the parameters weather, just one color, and graceful curves. I created this quilt in the middle of an oppressively hot Texas summer, so maybe I was wishing for cool, wet overcast days with majestic rolling clouds and rumbling thunder. I began with a relatively simple composition inspired by the Landscape Design Guide. Though I used mostly gray, I cheated a bit with the "just one color" requirement and added a bit of pale yellow embroidery to suggest the sun peeking through the clouds. You should feel free to cheat too!

Roll the Dice Art Quilt

DIE ROLL	THEME	COLOR PALETTE	DETAIL
1	Travel	Neutrals	Found-object stamped pattern (page 56)
2	Home	Blue, green, purple	Hand-embroidered filler stitch (page 67)
3	Illumination	Just one color	Positive and negative shapes (page 45)
4	Weather	Earth tones	Graceful curves stitched by machine (page 64)
5	Conversation	All the colors!	Freezer-paper stencil (page 54)
6	Cycles	Red, yellow, orange	Unexpected fabric such as upcycled clothing or sheer materials (page 18)

ASK YOURSELF

■ Was this exercise helpful? Or silly and contrived? (Is silly bad?)

■ What themes do you wish were listed in the chart? What colors?

■ Will you make a quilt based on these parameters?

■ Would your quilt be abstract or realistic?

■ What ideas popped into your head that were unexpected?

■ Did ideas flow easily? Or did you feel like you were really digging and searching?

gallery of student art quilt collages

I am lucky to have art quilter friends all over the world. Some are award-winning artists with years of experience. Some are finding their way into art quilting after years of making traditional quilts. I've met amazing people in my workshops. I love the connections I've made online— each of them inspires me in different ways. This network of friends is one of my favorite things about being an art quilter.

I've shared my techniques for creating an art quilt with layers of fabric, paint, and stitching—as well as the Eight Design Guides (page 22)—with many of them. They each interpreted the techniques and guides in their own way. This book is truly meant to be a framework for creating with fabric, paint, and stitching. These examples show the wide range of styles, techniques, ideas, and formats possible within this framework. Look for examples of sheer fabrics, interesting embellishments, complex hand stitching, free-motion quilting textures, unexpected color palettes, provocative symbols, and truly unique work!

in this chapter

✳ Check out inspiring examples of the Eight Design Guides.

✳ See art quilts with inspiring use of surface design, stitching, and personal symbols.

✳ Appreciate the personal style of many different art quilters.

✳ Get inspired to create your own original art quilt with fabric, paint, and stitching.

GALLERY OF THE EIGHT DESIGN GUIDES

Each of these artists used one of the Eight Design Guides as a prompt for creating an art quilt. Some of the quilts are direct interpretations and some are less obvious. The great thing about starting with one of the Eight Design Guides is that once you get started, you have a foundation for a composition that you can make your own in many ways.

Third Plus

Dragonfly Dance
by Tonya Littmann
14″ × 18″
tonyalittmann.blogspot.com

Tonya chose two beautifully dynamic fabrics for the one-third and two-thirds portions of the background. She used fabric painted with stenciled dragonflies for the "plus" part of the composition. Leaf shapes created with sheer fabrics add a bit of ethereal energy to the piece. Tonya says, "Dragonflies live in our pond. I noticed them the first time we saw our house. I thought they would bring us good luck. They are delicate and flirty and they make me happy." The small quilt is an unusual shape: a trapezium, meaning there are no parallel sides.

One Amazing Line

Hope
by Joanna Newman
9½″ × 10″
passionkiwi.com

Even though the whimsical red house takes center stage in this delightful small art quilt, the mysterious shape dripping into the chimney is a great example of One Amazing Line. Joanna says, "Hope is sometimes escaping its home, sneaking out the chimney to be chased or lost forevermore. Other times it is dripping, lavishly and abundantly, straight down from above." Joanna used a hand-embroidered chain stitch to outline the house and couched cords to emphasize the other shapes and lines in the quilt.

Symmetrical

Winter Dust
by VET
9″ × 12″
artcycletx.blogspot.com

Even though this tree has bare branches, it seems full of life. VET built a symmetrical composition with the tree in the center and the four leaf shapes continuing the balanced design. The background fabrics are layered like a landscape, making this an excellent example of combining two of the Design Guides—Symmetrical and Landscape. The hand embroidery adds another layer of interest and texture.

Modular

Lucky 8
by Lu Peters
11″ × 14″
lupeters.com

Just a few fabrics were used to create this sophisticated, calm design. Lu used the Modular Design Guide to carefully place each piece, thoughtfully overlapping fabrics to visually connect all the elements. Lu says she is influenced by Asian art and symbolism. She notes that "eight is the lucky symbol in Chinese culture that represents prosperity, health, and happiness." The fraying edges and gritty rust-dyed fabrics contrast with the clean lines of the deep red center rectangle to create a beautiful balance of textures.

Dancing Grid

Brought Forward
by Alisa Banks
16″ × 20″
alisabanks.com

The various fabrics, colors, and images work together because they are all squares and rectangles composed using the Dancing Grid Design Guide. Alisa chose intriguing imagery of clocks, handwriting, and blocks of text. The addition of the bold red line takes a bit of inspiration from the One Amazing Line Design Guide. Alisa says, "Lines often appear in my work to convey our connectedness to each other—our family and our communities and beyond."

Landscape

Grasses
by Candy Grisham
4½˝ × 9½˝

Candy chose a beautiful fabric palette and created a composition using the Landscape Design Guide, with different edge treatments for each layer. The landscape is somewhat abstract but still suggests a depth of view with a clear foreground and background. Wispy, wavy grasses cross over each layer. The machine stitching is complemented by just a few tiny hand-stitched lines and knots. The button embellishment picks up the circular motif from one of the fabrics. The shapes and colors are thoughtfully repeated throughout the design.

Magic Three

Black Magic Garden
by Beth Swider
18″ × 18″

Beth made a bold and unexpected choice by cutting these flower shapes from black felt. They work beautifully against the brightly colored layered background. The three flowers are carefully composed to create interest through their placement at different heights within the frame. Beth used free-motion machine quilting to stitch the words of Henri Matisse's quote, "There are always flowers for those who want to see them."

Grid

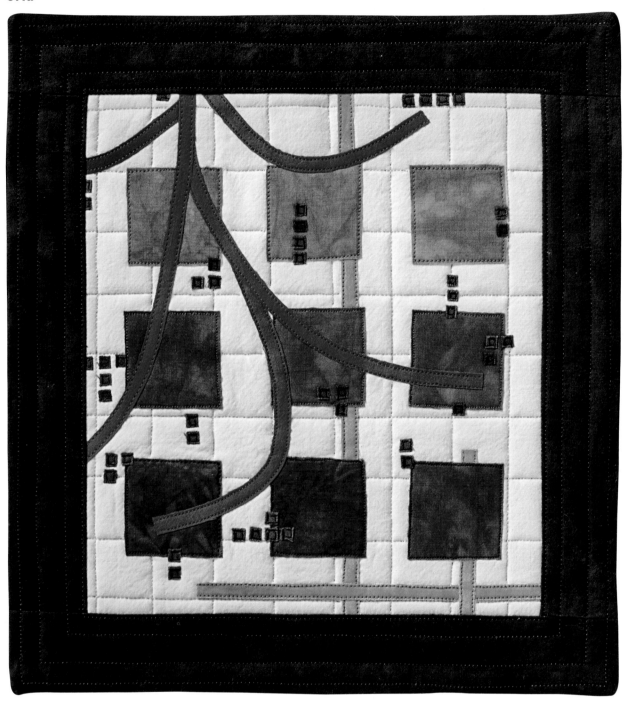

Line Dance
by Donna Akins
10½″ × 9½″

This is far from a typical nine-patch! Donna chose a spectrum of nine green fabrics and arranged them using the Grid Design Guide. They are beautifully complemented by tiny blue squares arranged in a random—yet balanced—configuration. The meandering red lines help draw the eye around the design, while the orange straight lines ground the piece by emphasizing the grid structure. The small quilt is framed with a border of deep purple. Even the machine-quilted stitching repeats the grid.

GALLERY OF ADDITIONAL TECHNIQUES

Surface Design

Mission Church, 8″ × 6″
and
2 Frames 2 Solids, 7½″ × 6″
by Amalia Parra Morusiewicz
FUNfromAtoZ.com

Amalia created a great collection of small art quilts combining commercial prints with her own original surface-designed fabrics. She used a variety of techniques, including printing with bubble wrap. Look closely to see the fabric stamped with an empty spool. There are also bits of fabric painted with watered-down acrylic paint. These are excellent examples of how a stash of fabric with your own original surface design gives your work flair and personality.

Personal Symbols

here
by Kristin
La Flamme
14˝ × 16˝
kristinlaflamme.com

Kristin often includes houses in her work. She says the houses in this quilt "are based on a drawing my son made of the row house we lived in at the time. They symbolize home and community and a bit of a nod to the European lifestyle I enjoy. Sometimes the houses in my work grow roots and evolve towards the idea of home and settling down (growing roots, or the inability to do so)." The composition is inspired by the Third Plus Design Guide, with a horizontal orientation. Kristin included stunning free-motion machine quilting to emphasize the roots and obsessive hand stitching to create the word "here."

Stitching

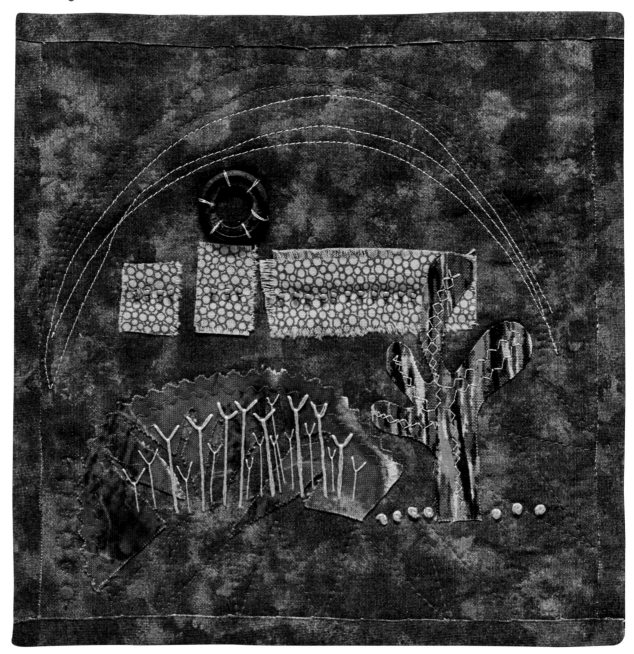

Fall After All
by Mary Masal
7″ × 7″

This small art quilt incorporates hand and machine stitching to create wonderful details. Mary even used a decorative machine stitch programmed in her sewing machine in the lower left. The arch and the diagonal stitching frame the tiny composition. The tall Y stitches add interest, and the color choices of floss and thread tie in with the fabrics. An old metal washer embellishes the scene. Mary loves to add found objects to her work. She wonders, "What use did they serve before they were found? How have they been reshaped by their journey through the streets?"

about the author

Photo by Sherrie Tootle

Deborah saves tiny scraps of cloth with unexpected bits of inspiring paint and ink. She picks up smashed bottle caps in parking lots and beautifully smooth stones at the beach. She appreciates peeling paint and scribbled notes as much as fine art and beautiful scenic vistas. She tries to embrace spontaneity and stability in equal measure. Her award-winning art quilts exemplify these varied interests and ideas.

Deborah has lived in twelve different states in nearly every part of the United States. In each home, she made a place to stitch and create, whether it was the dining room table, the unfinished basement, or her current in-home studio space. The personal symbols and details in her art quilts reflect her experiences and feelings about places she's lived and the things she's done. In her art quilts, the tiny details are as important as the overall design. As in life, little everyday joys compliment the bigger adventures.

Her art quilts have been exhibited in quilt shows and art galleries throughout the United States and internationally. She is published in many books and magazines. Deborah also created a DVD fabric collage workshop, teaches classes, and blogs about her artistic process.

Deborah regularly gives presentations and workshops to quilt guilds and visual arts groups. She is always eager to share her ideas about creativity and the possibilities of creating with fabric.

She gently nudges students to try new things as they work through the process of creating original art that they love.

Deborah and her husband, Jeff, live just outside of Dallas, Texas, with their two kids, Claire and Benjamin, and their lab mix, Lincoln. They are a nerdy, puzzle-loving, show-tune-singing, book-reading family who love to travel, learn new things, and eat ice cream.

Follow Deborah's art and creative life:

WEBSITE:
DeborahsStudio.com

BLOG:
DeborahsJournal.blogspot.com

FACEBOOK:
facebook.com/
DeborahBoschertArtist

INSTAGRAM:
instagram.com/deborahboschert/

TWITTER:
twitter.com/dhbosch

PINTEREST:
pinterest.com/d_boschert/

Twelve by Twelve: The International Art Quilt Challenge

I am a member of a group of artists called Twelve by Twelve: The International Art Quilt Challenge. Beginning in 2007, each of the twelve artists created 12″ × 12″ art quilts inspired by specific themes and color palettes. In 2012, we created our final series, changing the dimensions of our quilts to 20″ × 12″. It was a wonderfully collaborative, supportive, exciting, and fulfilling project. The art quilts I created as part of Twelve by Twelve are some of my very best work, and the friends I made are some of my most cherished.

All the quilts by the Twelve by Twelve artists can be seen on our website, twelveby12.org.

The following quilts included in this book are part of the original Twelve by Twelve collections.

Hibiscus, page 7: The ColorPlay Series; Orange color palette

Savory Scatterings, page 15: The ColorPlay Series; Spice color palette

Sugar Maple, page 17: The 2012 Series; Sweet theme

Spring Suggestion, page 28: The ColorPlay Series; Brown, Blue, and Sage color palette

Driving, page 36: The 2012 Series; Maverick theme

Yellow Ladder, page 41: The ColorPlay Series; Lorikeet color palette

Want even more creative content?

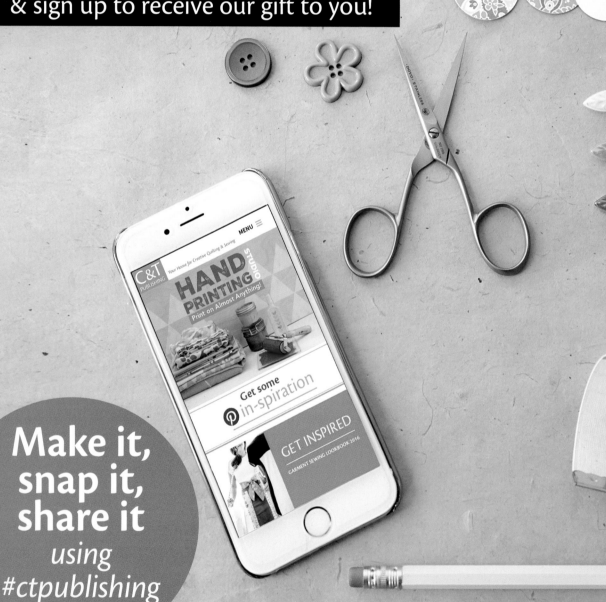

Make it, snap it, share it *using* *#ctpublishing*